The Book of Fate & Fortune
Cheiro's Numerology and Astrology

The magic of Numbers has fascinated man ever since he unravelled its deeper meaning and significance in fortune telling. The Science of Numerology explains the occult significance of numbers and their influence and relation to human life, and showing how to determine one's lucky or important numbers, the number value of one's name and place of living and propitious times for important transactions and decisions. The system of numerology as explained by Cheiro is easy to follow and needs no intricate mathematical calculations. This complete unabridged, authorised edition will make you your own numerologist and help you win popularity and save you from falling into the hands of charlatans, vagrants and unscrupulous fortune tellers.

Count Louis Hamon, better known as 'Cheiro' is regarded as the most successful palmist, numerologist and astrologer of this century. He was seriously initiated into the art of fortune telling when he came to India and lived with the Joshi family in Bombay. He was one of the first to translate and interpret in English the Hindu works of palmistry. Thereafter starting his practice and continuing his study and research he wrote remarkable books on palmistry, numerology and astrology in English.

"Readers are sure to benefit from this work and have a clear understanding of the science of number."

Jagjit Uppal

Also available
in
Orient Paperbacks

Cheiro's Palmistry: The Book of Fate & Fortune
Cheiro's You and Your Star: The Book of the Zodiac
Astrology For You/Shakuntala Devi
Astrology For All/Pt. Ashutosh Ojha
Numerology For All/Pt. Ashutosh Ojha

Indian Predictive Astrology/Prof. Vishnu Sharma

The Book of Fate & Fortune
Cheiro's
NUMEROLOGY
&
ASTROLOGY

Orient
Paperbacks
DELHI | MUMBAI | HYDERABAD

ISBN : 978-81-222-0046-1

The Book of Fate & Fortune:
Cheiro's Numerology & Astrology

Subject: Body, Mind & Spirit / Numerology

© Vision Books Pvt. Ltd.

1st Published 1987
22nd Printing 2014

Cover design by Vision Studio

Published by
Orient Paperbacks
(A division of Vision Books Pvt. Ltd.)
5A/8 Ansari Road, New Delhi-110 002
www.orientpaperbacks.com

Printed at
Anand Sons, Delhi-110 092, India

Cover Printed at
Ravindra Printing Press, Delhi-110 006. India

Contents

Introduction by Jagjit Uppal — 9

Foreword by Cheiro — 15

1. The Planetary Numbers of the Months — 27

2. The Single Number—Their Meaning and Their Influence on Men and Women — 32
   Number 1; Number 2; Number 3; Number 4; Number 5; Number 6; Number 7; Number 8; & Number 9

3. The Occult Symbolism of 'Compound' Numbers With Illustrations — 68

4. The 'Compound' or 'Spiritual' Numbers Fully Described — 78

5. More Information on How to Use 'Single' and 'Compound' Numbers — 90

6. Why the Birth Number is the Most Important — 93

7. Some Illustrations of Names and Numbers — 96

8. Examples of How Numbers Recur in Lives — 98

9. The Dread of the '13' Unfounded — 101

10. The Extraordinary Example of Numbers in the Lives of St. Louis and Louis XVI — 104

11. Periodicity in Numbers — 107

12.	Some Additional Information	111
13.	How to Find the 'Lucky' Day	115
14.	Colours and Numbers	118
15.	The Value of Concentration in Regard to One's Number	121
16.	Combination Between 1 Hyphen 4 Persons and Numbers 4 and 8	124
17.	More Information About Persons Born Under the Numbers 4 and 8	127
18.	The Affinity of Colours and Numbers and How Music and Numbers are Associated	132
19.	Numbers and Disease: Planetary Significane of Herbal Cures	135
20.	How to Know What City, Town or Place is Fortunate for One to Live in	141
21.	Horse-Racing and Numbers	148
22.	Examples from the Names of Some Presidents of the United States	150
23.	The Bible and Numbers	156
24.	Astrology and Astrological Numbers	159

24. i) Basic Traits of Character of People Born in January; ii) Basic Traits of Character of People Born in February; iii) Basic Traits of Character of People Born in March; iv) Basic Traits of Character of People Born in April; v) Basic Traits of Character of People Born in May; vi) Basic Traits of Character of People Born in

June; vii) Basic Traits of Character of People Born in July; viii) Basic Traits of Character of People Born in August; ix) Basic Traits of Character of People Born in September; x) Basic Trait of Character of People Born in October; xi) Basic Traits of Character of People Born in November; xii) Basic Traits of Character of People Born in December

25. Occult Significance of Numbers with Birth Dates   205

26. Life's Triangles and Affinities   208

27. Lucky Colours and How to Know Them   217

Introduction
By Jagjit Uppal*

AS A PROFESSIONAL ASTROLOGER, I must admit that even though I studied astrology and palmistry in great depth, it was per chance I discovered the magic of numbers during the course of my learning. This ancient science of numbers has always fascinated mankind but only few have been able to unravel its deeper meaning and significance. Hindu seers contemplate on *Shoonya*, *Bindu* or zero, described variously as void, the beginning, or even one without beginning, self-effulgent, etc., and in this void they seek the self the ONE, the ominipresent which, numerologically, is represented as ONE. This itself is the gist of entire science of numbers 0 to 1. In modern times, we are aware of the importance of these two digits in computer language. But seers of yore were intuitively aware of the importance of these numbers and made remarkable study of numbers and their influence over life and events on earth. Such studies were usually shrouded in secrecy and hence it was a practice not to record or write one's observations lest these fall into the hands of uninitiated who could misuse such knowledge which gave unbounded power to its knower. As a result the finer aspects of the science of numbers have been lost in time. Apart from the Hindus, the ancient civilisations in Greece and Latin America, the practice of numerology was widespread. The Chaldeans, Hebrews, Egyptians, are known to have practiced

---

*Jagjit Uppal is a Bombay based renowned astrologer-palmist.

numerology.

Coming back to my own ignorance of this subject, I dismissed it earlier as elementary as far as occult discipline was concerned. For, I had by then, learned astrology whereby one's birth-chart revealed all about one's nature and life. I even marvelled at the lines on one's hand which to me, began to show clearly one's course of life. But, as I mentioned earlier, it was per chance that I discovered for myself the strange recurrence of certain numbers in my life, that I decided to delve more into this mysterious subject. And today I daresay that without the combined knowledge of Astrology, Palmistry and Numerology, the art of fortune telling would be incomplete. Here however, I will restrict myself to speaking about numerology, but we must not forget the importance of the entire philosophy of *Karma*, or the knowledge of universe, to understand the correspondence or co-relation between heavenly bodies, and the life on earth.

While learning astrology my first interest quite naturally, was to understand my own birth-chart. After learning the basics, once I asked my master if I was born a few minutes later, would everything change. To which he replied that there was no 'ifs' in our lives. Even your name, your environment, and personality, is governed by universal law. A too far fetched statement I presumed. But subsequently, I reaslied that, somehow, I was always getting associated with the number 7. To begin with, my moon is in Libra, 7th sign of the Zodiac. It is in the constellations *Vishakha*, which is the 16th, $1+6=7$, of the 27 constellations. I lived with my father in house No. 7. During holidays, I would visit my grandfather in Delhi who lived in house No. 16, again 7, in New Delhi-16. Several years later, when many zonal numbers in Delhi had changed, and my family had also moved house, we again found ourselves in zone No. 16. I can recount endless recurrence of this number in my life and this set me to go deeper into the mystery of numbers. And slowly, I must admit, I found numerology as accurate as artrology and palmistry, for forecasting. And in many ways it seemed easier and surer way to know one's personality and destiny. For, there could be several interpretations or understanding of a particular symbol on one's palm, whereas if one is governed by number 1 or 7, there is no two opinions about it. However, it is not all that simple either, for it takes a life long study to arrive at a simple thing like knowing one's destiny number. In the present work the author has gone into great detail in explaining the basic principles of numerology and how to calculate one's number of destiny.

About the author, I am sure most of the readers are fully acquainted with his name and works on fortune telling. Cheiro, born as Count Louis Hamon, came to India to study Palmistry and later set up his practice in London. During the course of his long career as a professional palmist, he had the privilege of meeting innumerable celebrities including kings, queens, ministers and artistes. One of his earlier clients was King Edward VII, then Prince of Wales. The Prince was born on 9th November. Cheiro describes his meeting with the Prince in his memoirs. He told the Prince that number 9 was significant in his life. The month of November is called in astrology "The Second House of Mars" and is governed by number 9. Thereafter Cheiro went into great detail in explaining how number 9 will play a very significant role in Edward's life. Through compound numbers he even discovered number 6 also as highly significant for Edward VII. We know that King Edward's marriage took place in the year 1863 which is $1+8+6+3=18=9$. He was to be crowned on 27 June which is 9 and 6. Though he was actually crowned on 9th August. After listening with rapt attention to Cheiro, King Edward himself indicated the year 69 saying "As this is the only date when these two curious numbers first come together, which you say are the key notes of my life, I suppose that must be the end?"

Such is the magic of numbers that inadvertently, the King had picked out the year of his death with uncanny precision. For the Fate did ordain King's death in his 69th year.

Cheiro explains that the month of April in which King Edward was afflicted with his fatal illness has from time immemorial been represented by the number 9. The month of May, in which he died, is similarly represented by a 6. The addition of the two figures of the age 69 equals $15=1+5=6$. He passed away on May 6th. Cheiro describes several such instances which proves the accuracy of the system of numerology. The present volume has been written in a very simple language and Cheiro has explained in detail the meanings of each number as also certain compound numbers. The Chapter on Names and Numbers will also interest readers and they may profit by adding or deleting letters which can help or harm their interests. This raises a very pertinent question, "Can we change our destiny?" If we have the knowledge of numerology and know that a certain number is negative for us, can we avoid its maleficence. I would like to render a brief explanation on this subject, though the scope of this foreward limits me from going into greater detail and the subject of Fate and Freewill is a matter which would by itself constitute one volume.

We are aware that our birth is without our choice. So is our parentage and circumstances. The theory of Genetics has proved that the genes define our personality. Our responses to life situations depend upon our personality and environment, and over both these we have no control. We can only understand our responses. And lastly, the only certainty that exists in our future is death. Hence our very existence that is birth and death, is choiceless. It is our Ego which makes it difficult to accept that we are puppets in the hands of Fate. Albert Camus, a French existentialist philosopher, when confronted by such ideas was very disturbed and somehow could not accept them. But then he had no choice over his birth and environment. Then he hit upon a brilliant idea. That at least he is free to choose his moment of death. That itself would prove his freedom. But a beliver in pre-destination questioned him that if he would let him know in advance when will he die. Camus said there was enough time to make such plans. For the time, Camus had won his argument. But Fate willed it otherwise. Albert Camus was not given the chance or freedom to choose his end, for he met with an accident and died.

Those who know astrology and palmistry are well aware that suicidal tendencies are clearly indicated in one's horoscope and in the lines on the hand. So astrologers and palmists will not agree that if man took his or other's life, he has asserted his choice. They would say he was Fated to do so.

Some astrologers believe that planets and lines on hands indicate trends and not certainties. This is a contradiction. For if we cannot say with certainty what is in store for us in the Future, then there is hardly any need to study such subjects. Does that mean that every thing is pre-destined and we cannot alter anything? Isn't this frightening to know that we are helpless tools in the hands of Fates? Is that the reason such subjects are shrouded in mystery and secrecy so as not to cause alarm and fear in the uninitiated? I leave readers to ponder over these points and come to their own conclusions. But I must add that as long as we do not know accurately, what lies in future, there is scope for us to use free will, choice or discrimination to lead our lives. And we are well aware, that no amount of learning can give us insight into the furture completely. And this must be the reason that ancient *Rishis* and seers, kept this knowledge a secret.

However, to conclude, we must not forget that to know oneself is the highest learning. And if astrology, palmistry or numerology can help us understand ourselves better, we will surely be able to conduct our lives in a more orderly manner. Similarly, the knowledge of numerology helps us to have more understanding and compassion towards others and accept them as they are. Readers are sure to benefit from this work and have a clear understanding of the Science of Numbers.

Foreword

DURING MY EARLIER YEARS, when travelling in the East, it had been my good fortune to come in contact with a certain sect of Brahmins who had kept in their hands from almost prehistoric times studies and practices of an occult nature which they regarded as sacredly as they did their own religious teachings. Among other things, they permitted me to learn certain theories on the occult significance of numbers and their influence and relation to human life, which subsequent years and manifold experiences not only confirmed, but justified me in endeavouring to apply them in a practical sense so that others might also use this knowledge with, I hope, advantage to themselves and to those around them.

The ancient Hindu searchers after Nature's laws, it must be remembered, were in former years masters of all such studies, but in transmitting their knowledge to their descendants, they so endeavoured to hide their secrets from the common people that in most cases the key to the problem became lost, and the truth that had been discovered became buried in the dust of superstition and charlatanism, to be re-formed, let us hope, when some similar cycle of thought in its own appointed time will again claim attention to this side of nature.

This ancient people, together with the Chaldeans and Egyptians, were the absolute masters of the occult or hidden meaning of numbers, in their application to time and in their relation to human life.

It was the Hindus who discovered the precession of the Equinoxes, and their calculation that such an occurrence takes places every 25,827 years; only later to be proved correct by modern science after labours of hundreds of years.

It is impossible here to give in detail all the reasonings and examples that exist for a belief in the occult side of numbers, but it may interest my readers if I give a few illustrations of why the number 7 has for ages been regarded as *the number of mystery relating to the spirtual side of things*, and why the number 9 has in its turn come to be regarded as the *finality or end of the series on which all our materialistic calculations are built*, but the most casual observer can only admit that beyond the number 9 all ordinary numbers become but a mere repitition of the first 9. A simple illustration of this will readily suffice. The number 10, as the zero is not a number, becomes a repetition of the number 1. The number 11 added together as the ancient occultists laid down in their law of *natural addition*, namely, adding together from left to right, repeats the number 2, 12 repeats 3, 13 repeats 4, and so on up to 19, which in its turn becomes 1 plus 9 equals 10, and so again the repetition of 1. 20 represents 2, and so on to infinity. The occult symbolism of what are called compound numbers, that is, those numbers from 10 onwards, I will explain later.

In this way it will be seen that in all our *materialistic* systems of numbers, the number 1 to 9 are the base on which we are compelled to build, just as in the same way the seven great or primary harmonies in music are the bases of all music, and again as the seven primary colours are the bases of all our combinations of colours.

In the most ancient rules of occult philosophy we find

the rule laid down that the number 7 *is the only number capable of dividing 'the number of Eternity'*, and continuing in itself as long as the number representing Eternity lasts, and yet, *at every addition of itself producing the number 9*, or in other words it produces the basic numbers on which all materialistic calculations are built and on which all human beings depend and the whole edifice of human thought finds expression.

Example

The number 1 is the first number. It represents the First Cause, Creator, God, or Spirit, call it as you like. A circle or the zero, 'O', has always been taken as the symbol of endlessness—otherwise Eternity. Place the 1 and the figure zero by its side, and you get the significant symbol of eternity such as 1 plus 0, the 10, and then, place as many of these emblems of eternity side by side as you like, and you get such a figure as 1,00,000. Divide by the mystic number 7 and you get the number 142857.

$$\frac{7)1,000,000}{142857}$$

Add as many zeros as you like, and keep on dividing by the 7, and you yourself may go on through all eternity and you can only get repetitions of the same 142857, which from time immemorial has been called the 'sacred number'. Now add this number wherever you find it by natural addition, it will give you the figure 27, and as you have seen by the rule of natural addition described on a preceding page, you keep adding till only one number remains, to arrive at what is known as 'the root of the number.' You add again 27 by natural addition, and 2 plus 7 equals 9, or in other words, you get the full range of the first series of numbers on which all *materialistic or human calculations can be built.*

Now, let us return to the symbolism of seven for a moment. You know, of course, that Buddha is always represented as sitting in the centre of a Lotus. Let us examine, then, the secret of such a selection. It is not perhaps generally known that the 7 is reproduced in many strange ways in Nature herself, and that flowers that have *not been crossed* by intermingling with other flowers have their outside petals in the number of seven, but as flowers are so easily crossed with other varieties, and it is so difficult to find a pure type, Buddha took the Lotus, which never becomes crossed or loses its individuality, as the emblem of the religion he taught, because, first, its seven foundation petals are always in evidence, and further, the religion he taught was that the creative Spirit was the foundation and origin of all things, and thus again bore silent but unmistakable testimony to the creative action of the seven planets from which all religions have had their origin.

Long before man made his creeds, or civilisations their laws, the influence of these seven planets had become known on the earth. Out of the dark night of antiquity their light became law and as far as we can penetrate, even to the very confines of prehistoric days, in all races, in all countries, we find the influence of the seven planets through all and in all.

Days of The Week

The seven days of the week have been the outcome of the influence of the seven creative planets and gave the names of the days of the week, in every land or clime. Take any nation you may choose, this fact remains the same, and is so expressed in almost every language, Chinese, Assyrian, Hindi, Egyptian, Hebrew. Greek, Latin, French, German, or English.

We know today that the heavenly bodies move through their orbits with such precision that in millions of years they do not vary one minute of time. We know that they exercise an influence on this earth which is felt by the veriest atoms in the earth, though what this force is, or with what incredible speed it acts, may forever remain a mystery. It was in dealing with this mysterious law that the ancient philosopher by study, experiments, concentration of mind, and perhaps intuition, arrived at the fixation of certain laws governing life, which may be as accurate as their discovery that the 'precession of the Equinoxes takes place once in every 25,827 years.'

It is from these wonderful students of nature that we have received the first idea as to the divisions of the Zodiac into twelve periods of 30 degrees, and further, that each period produces a definite and well-known influence on the earth and on human beings born in any of its twelve periods. They further subdivided these 30-degree periods into division of three periods of 10 degrees each, in which the planets are also found to have an influence, and they pursued their investigations until they worked out a system demonstrating that each day had its own particular meanings due to vibrations in the ether, which keeps the earth in instantaneous report with its entire solar system, and lastly, that as the sun enters a new degree of the Zodiac in mid-winter at about the rate of every $2\frac{1}{2}$ to 3 minutes, and the summer at the rate of 3 to $4\frac{3}{4}$ minutes, that its magnetic influence varied the effect of the vibrations or ether waves of each planet, and so enable these students of Nature to carry their system in this way down to almost the smallest fraction of time.[1]

---

[1] This applies, of course, to the motion of the sun through the symbolic or cabbalistic Zodiac used in the East.

In examining this subject, let us take for an example a clock. Keeping this in your mind for a moment let us regard the 360 degrees of the Zodiac into which the sun appears to pass, from degree to degree on an average of every 4 minutes as the teeth of one of our wheels. This 360 degrees multiplied by the 4 minutes gives 1,440 minutes, and this, divided by 60, to bring it to hours, gives us the 24-hour day, which becomes in its turn another spoke in the great wheel of time, and consequently, by the advance of the sun, must bring us to the commencement of another day *under new and distinct influences, and so on until the year itself is completed.*

Now as science proves that it takes the sun 30 days to pass from one division of the Zodiac into another, again we have the illustration of another wheel, as it were, but a still slower one being put into motion, and consequently with the change in the heavenly mechanism another set of influences are brought to bear upon the earth, and so on until the twelve months of the year have in their turn experienced the influence of the sun in the twelve divisions of the Zodiac.

Let us now return for a moment to the part played by the seven creative planets. No-one today, I believe, can plead ignorance of the effect of one of these planets, namely the moon on the earth itself and on the people who inhabit the earth. We all know, or at least have heard, about the effect of the moon on the brain of people mentally unbalanced. We know how it causes tides to rise and fall along our shores, but still perhaps we do not realise that even in the deepest ocean its pull or attraction is so great that it causes hundreds of thousands of tons of dead weight of water to be drawn up by it to such a height as 70 feet in the Bay of Fundy and in the Bristol Channel.

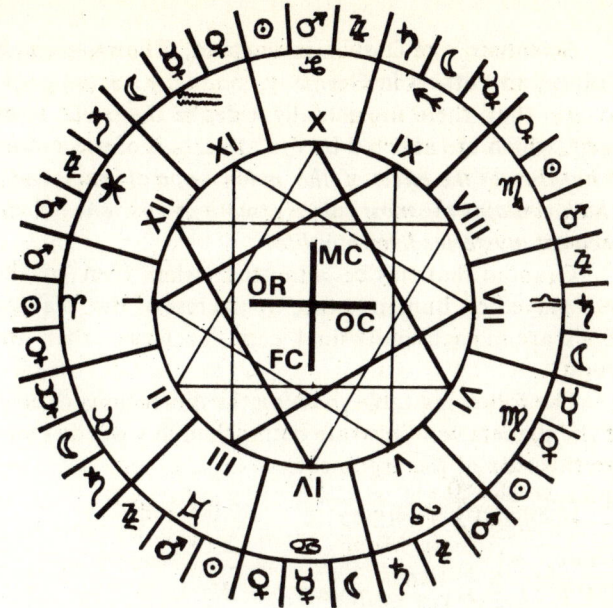

Fig. 1

Map showing the Twelve Divisions of the Zodiac, each division sub-divided into three parts of 10 degrees.

SIGNS OF THE ZODIAC
 I. Aris ethe Ram
 II. Taurus, the Bull
 III. Gemini, the Twins
 IV. Cancer, the Crab
 V. Leo, the Lion
 VI. Virgo, the Virgin
 VII. Libra, the Balance
 VIII. Scorpio, the Scorpion
 IX. Sagittarius, the Archer
 X. Capricorn, the Goat
 XI. Aquarius, the Water-Bearer
 XII. Pisces, the Fishes

This map represents the Sun's entry into Aries in the Vernal Equinox on March 21-23 of every year. The letters at the points of the central cross stand for: **OR**—Oriental or Eastern; **MC**—Mid-Heaven; **OC**—Occidental or Western; **FC**—Lower **Heaven.**

Scientists, like Darwin in England, Flammarion in France, and others in Germany, made the startling discovery that there are actually tides *in the solid earth itself*, which are affected by the attraction of the moon *What then of the effect of the moon on the brain itself, which contains the most subtle essence and is one of the greatest mysteries known in life.*

Granted that this be admitted, what then of the part played on human nature by the rest of the planets, which are in each individual case far larger than the moon?

The following table showing the dimensions of each of the planets will illustrate better than any words I may use this side of the argument.

Diameter of		
Mercury	2,000	miles
the Moon	2,100	,,
Venus	7,510	,,
the Earth	7,913	,,
Mars	4,920	,,
Jupiter	88,390	,,
Saturn	71,900	,,
Uranus	33,000	,,
Neptune	36,000	,,
the Sun	860,000	,,

I ask, is it logical, with such a demonstration before one, to admit the effect of the moon and to deny any effect to the other planets that are in fact so much larger than it?

Let us now return to the important side of the question as regards the rules set forth in this book. You will very naturally ask, how and when were such numbers arrived at that represent the mechanical action or influence of the celestial system on the people of this earth? I could write an entire volume on this side of the

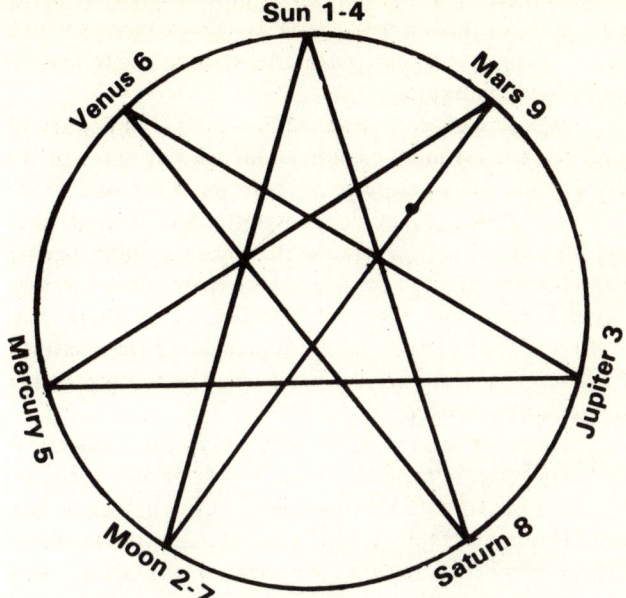

Fig. 2 : The Explanation of Seven-Pointed Seal of Solomon

The Sun, with the numbers 1 hyphen 4, represents the combination of the Sun and the planet Uranus (the male quality of Creation being the Sun with the feminine Uranus *of the mental or spiritual plane*) The Moon, with the numbers 2 hyphen 7, represents the Moon and Neptune, the Moon being feminine on the material or earth plane with Neptune (masculine) *on the mental or spiritual plane.*

The meaning of the lines of the Star being: That Life starts from the Sun—proceeds to the Moon, from that to Mars, from Mars to Mercury, Mercury to Jupiter, Jupiter to Venus, Venus to Saturn, and from Saturn (symbol of death) it returns to the Sun—or God from whence it came—to begin all over again in another cycle, *and so on through eternity.*

question alone, but in the following necessarily condensed pages you will find the general law explained which may be sufficient to elucidate the system contained in the following chapters.

In the first place, the secret or occult significance of numbers was revealed to man so far back in the world's history that the exact place of their discovery has never been recorded, but it suffices to state that if one goes back in one's investigations to the most distant period in the history of any race who made themselves in any degree responsible for such studies, even there one would find that these numbers representing the qualities of the solar system and the basis of all our later forms of calculation existed.

In working out the idea contained in these pages, I have carefully investigated every important form of occultism bearing on this question, but whether it has been Hindu, Egyptian, Chaldean, or Greek, the symbols of these numbers have always appeared the same, and their relation to months, days, hours, and people representing certain numbers, has been more or less alike.

What is called 'the secondary numbers' as illustrated on subsequent pages I myself have brought into a practical form, but they have in every case been built up from long investigation and experience extending over many years. Although we may never be able to find out the exact time in past ages when the influence of these numbers was discovered, that is no reason why we should not accept what has been given us by those ancient students.

The origin of life we know not, but we are none the less conscious that life exists. The balance, poise, and hidden laws governing our own solar system have also never been explained, together with a thousand other things in our everyday life. The very origin of numbers is itself a mystery; yet we are forced to employ them, and as Balzac says, 'without them, the whole edifice of our civilisation would fall to pieces.'

In the Book of the Wisdom of Solomon, now included in the Apocrypha, Solomon says:

For God Himself gave me an urerring knowledge of the things that are, to know the constitution of the world, the begginning and the end end and middle of times, the alterations of the solstices, the chages of seasons and the positions of the planets, the nature of living creatures and the thoughts of men, all things that are either secret or manifest I learned, for He that is the artificer of all things taught me this wisdom.

I ask, could anything be more forcible or convincing than such a statement, particularly when it is remembered that the true Seal of Solomon was none other than the seven-pointed star which contained the nine numbers which constitute the base of all our calculations, and which is the root of the system of numbers as applied to human life?

Even in our chemistry we have given a number and symbol to all the elements,

Water is	1010 its symbol is H_2O
Hydrogen	212 its symbol is H
Oxygen	1030 its symbol is O
Nitrogen	1969 its symbol is N
Carbon	1050 its symbol is C

and so on.

All occult studies point to the fact that the ancient students had a foundation for ascribing to every human being *his number in the universe*, and if we admit, as we do, that there is a moment for birth and a moment for death, so also in the links of years, days, and hours, that make up the chain of life, it is not illogical to assume that *every link of life has also both its number and place.* I claim that by such a study man may become more perfect by his fitting in with the laws, system, and order of things to which he owes his being.

There is evidence that those ancient students were conversant with the fact that there were two more distant planets than Saturn in our solar system, for they assigned beyond 'the seven creative planets' the orbits for two more heavenly bodies, and they described them as governing the thoughts *on the mental side of Nature* and not the physical, and their description of them is in exact accordance with our present-day knowledge of the effect of the recently discovered planets of Uranus and Neptune on human life.

CHEIRO

1

The Planetary Numbers of The Months

ALTHOUGH LATER IN these pages the reader will find how the single and compound numbers have each their particular meaning in connection with human life, it is well at this stage to understand how and why the months have received their particular numbers.

The true solar year commences with the Sun's entrance into the Vernal or Spring Equinox on the 21st to the 23rd day of March of every year, and appears to pass through each Sign of the Zodiac of 30 degrees each, one after the other, taking slightly under $365\frac{1}{4}$ days in so doing, making our year popularly accepted as 365 days.

The Earth, revolving, once upon its own axis each 24 hours, causes the whole of the 13 Signs of the Zodiac in their turn to pass over each portion of the Earth once each 24 hours The Moon revolves round the Earth in a lunar month of 28 days. This wonderful mechanism, if I may call it so, is exactly like the hour-hand, minute-hand, and second-hand of a clock.

What is called the first sign of the Zodiac is the 'period of the number 9' or the Zodiacal *Sign of Aries*, from the 21st March to the 19th April. It is ruled by the Planet Mars in its *positive* aspect, and has the 9 for its number.

The 'period of the number 6' is the Zodiacal *Sign of Taurus* from the 20th April to the 20th May. It is ruled by the Planet Venus in its *positive* aspect, and has the 6 for its number.

The 'period of the number 5' is the Zodiacal *Sign of Gemini*, from the 21st May to the 20th June. It is ruled by the Planet Mercury in its *positive* aspect, and has the 5 for its number.

The 'period of the 2 and 7' is the Zodiacal *Sign of Cancer*, from the 21st June to the 20th July. It is ruled by the Moon in its *positive* aspect, and has the double figure of 2—7 for its number.

The 'period of the 1 and 4' is the Zodiacal *Sign of Leo*, from the 21st July to the 20th August. It is ruled by the Sun in its *positive* aspect, and has the double figures of 1—4 for its number.

The 2nd 'period of the number 5' is the Zodiacal *Sign of Virgo* from the 21st August to the 20th September. It is ruled by the Planet Mercury in its *negative* aspect, and has the 5 for its number.

The 2nd 'period of the number 6' is the Zodiacal *Sign of Libra* from the 21st September to the 20th October. It is ruled by the Planet Venus in its *negative* aspect, and has the 6 for its number.

The 2nd 'period of the number 5' is the Zodiacal *Sign of Scorpio* from the 21st October to the 20th November. It is ruled by the Planet Mars in its *negative* aspect, and has the 9 for its number.

The 'period of the number 3' is the Zodiacal *Sign of Sagittarius*, from the 21st November to 20th December. It is ruled by the Planet Jupiter in its *positive* aspect, and has the 3 for its number.

The 'period of the number 8' is the Zodiacal *Sign of Capricorn*, from the 21st December to the 20th January. It is ruled by the Planet Saturn in its *positive* aspect, and has the 8 for its number.

The 2nd 'period of the number 8' is the Zodiacal

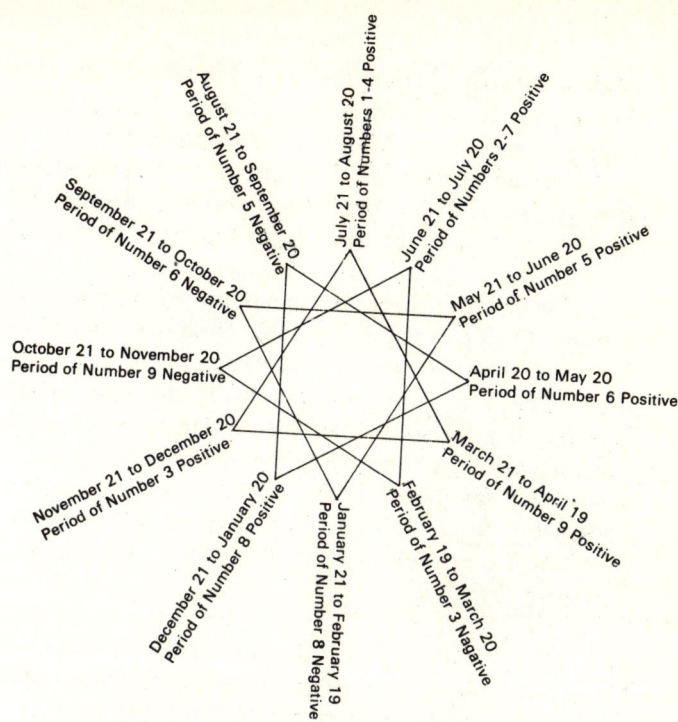

Fig. 3 : The Four Divisions of the Zodiac
Fire, Water, Air and Earth

THE FIRE TRIANGLE
1st "House," March 21 to April 19.
2nd "House," July 21 to August 20
3rd "House," November 21 to December 20.
THE AIR TRIANGLE
1st "House," May 21 to June 20.
2nd "House," September 21 to October 20.
3rd "House," January 21 to February 19.
THE WATER TRIANGLE
1st "House," June 21 to July 20.
2nd "House," October 21 to November 20.
3rd "House," February 19 to March 20.
THE EARTH TRIANGLE
1st "House," April 20 to May 20.
2nd "House," August 21 to September 20.
3rd "House," December 21 to January 20

Sign of Aquarius, from the 21st January to the 21st February. It is ruled by the Planet Saturn in its *negative* aspect, and has the 8 for its number.

The 2nd 'period of the number 3' is the Zodiacal *Sign of Pisces*, from the 19th February to the 20th March. It is ruled by the Planet Jupiter in its *negative* aspect, and has the 3 for its number.

This brings us back to the point from where we started. Owing to the Sun passing from one Sign of the Zodiac to another, seven days are allowed at the beginning of each sign and seven days at the end, which is called the 'Cusp of the Sign'; during this period the number of the month and the qualities it represents *are not quite so strong* as during the rest of the period, and partakes to a certain extent *of the qualities of the Sign which is passing away* with those of the one *that is coming into action*.

It will be observed that the Planets have a Positive and Negative quality in accordance with the period of the Zodiac they rule; the Positive giving the more physical and forceful qualities, the Negative the mental.

For example, the symbol of the 9 *positive* in the Sign of Aries is: A man in armour with his visor closed and a naked sword in his hand.

The 9 *negative* in the Sign of Scorpio is represented by a man also in armour, but with the visor up showing his face, and the sword in its sheath, giving the picture of the mental warrior rather than the physical.

The Sun and the Moon are the only two Planets having what is called 'double numbers,' because the Sun and Uranus are interrelated to one another, so the number of the Sun is written as 1—4.

The Moon being interrelated with Neptune is written as 2—7.

A curious thing, and one well worth noting, is that there appears to be a sympathy and attraction between the numbers 1—4 and 2—7, and it will be found that persons born under any of the 1—4 numbers, such as the 1st, 4th, 10th, 13th, 19th, 22nd, 28th, and 31st, are sympathetic and get on well with people born under the numbers 2—7, such as the 2nd, 7th, 11th, 16th, 20th, 25th, and 29th and more especially so if either of these two sets of people is born in the 'House of the Moon,' namely between the 20th June and July 21st—27th, or in the 'House of the Sun,' between the 21st July and August 20th—27th.[1]

THE NUMBERS GIVEN TO THE DAYS OF THE WEEK ARE AS FOLLOWS:

Sunday	1—4	Thursday	3
Monday	2—7	Friday	6
Tuesday	9	Saturday	8
Wednesday	5		

These numbers correspond to the Planets as follows.

Sun	1	Venus	6
Moon	2	Neptune	7
Jupiter	3	Saturn	8
Uranus	4	Mars	9
Mercury	5		

---

[1] I have added the seven days of the 'Cusp' to each of these periods.

2

The Single Numbers—Their Meaning and Their Influence on Men and Women

THERE IS NO GETTING away from the fact that there are only nine Planets in our Solar System, also that *there are only nine numbers by which all our calculations on this Earth are made*. Beyond these nine numbers all the rest are repetitions, as 10 is a 1 with a zero added, an 11 is 1 plus 1, a 2; a 12 is 1 plus 2, a 3; and so on; every number, no matter how high, can be reduced to a single figure by what is called 'natural addition' from *left to right*. The final single number that remains is called the 'spirit or soul number' of all the previous numbers added together.

In this first part of this study there are only nine numbers to be considered, and one has but to master the occult meaning of each of these nine numbers as they occur in the Birth dates of men and women to find a Key to secrets of human nature that open a source of amazing interest.

I will endeavour to write as simply as possible that all who read may clearly understand what these numbers mean, even in the most everyday actions of life.

Without going into any elaborate description of why this or that influence has been given to any particular number, I will without more preamble go straight to the subject, and show how each person may find what their number may be and how they may utilise this information.

The nine numbers we have got to study are: 1, 2, 3, 4, 5, 6, 7, 8, and 9. These numbers were given to the Planets that control our system in the most distant ages of civilisation, and have been used and adopted by all students of occultism, Chaldean, Hindu, Egyptian, or Hebrew.

The secret underlying the whole of this idea is that of the mysterious law of vibration. The day of Birth giving a Key number that is related to the Planet bearing the same number, this representing a vibration that lasts all through life, and which may, or may not, be in accord with the 'Name number,' which I will explain later, and with the vibrations of individuals with whom we are brought into contact.

First we must consider each number in relation to the Planet it—if I may use a simple expression—represents.

The Number 1

The number 1 stands in this symbolism for the Sun. It is the beginning—that by which all the rest of the nine numbers were created. The basis of all numbers is *one*—the basis of all life is *one*. This number represents all that is creative, individual, and positive. Without going into further details, a person born under the Birth number of 1, or any of its series, has the underlying principles of being in his or her work creative, inventive, strongly individual, definite in his or her views, and in consequence more or less obstinate and determined in all they as individuals undertake. This relates to all men and women born under the number 1, such as on the 1st, 10th, 19th, or 28th of any month (the addition of all these numbers making a 1), but more especially so if they happen to be born between the 21st July and the 28th August, which is the period of the Zodiac called the 'House of the Sun,' or from the 21st March to the 28th April, when the Sun enters the Vernal Equinox and is considered elevated or all-powerful during this period. It is for this reason, which you will observe has a logical basis, that people born under the number 1 in *these particular periods* must have the qualities that I have given to all number 1 people *in a distinctly more marked degree*.

Number 1 people are ambitious; they dislike restraint, they always rise in whatever their profession or occupation may be. They desire to become the heads of whatever their businesses are, and as departmental chiefs they keep their authority and make themselves respected and 'looked up to' by their subordinates.

These number 1 people should endeavour to carry out their most important plans and ideas on all days that vibrate to their own number, such as on the 1st, 10th, 19th, or 28th of any month, but especially in those periods I have described before, namely, from the 21st July to the 28th August, and from the 21st March to the 28th April. Outside of their own numbers, number 1 people get on well with persons born under the 2, 4, and 7, such as those born on the 2nd, 4th, 7th, 11th, 13th, 16th, 20th, 22nd, 25th, 29th, and 31st, especially those born in *the strong periods indicated*.

The days of the week most fortunate for number 1 persons are Sunday and Monday, and especially so if one of their 'own numbers' should also fall on that day, such as the 1st, 10th, 19th, or 28th, and next to that their interchangeable numbers of 2, 4, 7, such as the 2nd, 4th, 7th, 11th, 13th, 16th, 20th, 22nd, 25th, 29th, or 31st.

The most fortunate colours for persons born under the number 1 are all shades of gold, yellows and bronze to golden brown.

Their 'lucky' jewels are the topaz, amber, yellow diamond, and all stones of these colours.

If possible, they should wear a piece of amber next their flesh.

Famous People Born Under the Number 1

Alexander the Great	Born	1st July	Represents	1
James 1	,,	28th June	,,	1
Charles I	,,	19th Nov.	,,	1
George I	,,	28th May	,,	1
George II	,,	10th Oct.	,,	1
Duke of Wellington	,,	1st May	,,	1
General Gordon	,,	28th Jan.	,,	1
President Garfield	,,	19th Nov.	,,	1
'General' Booth	,,	10th April	,,	1
Field-Marshal Earl Haig	,,	19th June	,,	1
Queen Alexandra	,,	1st Dec.	,,	1
Field-Marshal Lord French	,,	28th Sept.	,,	1
David Livingstone	,,	19th Mar.	,,	1
Lord Charles Beresford	,,	10th Feb.	,,	1
Annie Besant	,,	1st Oct.	,,	1
President Wilson	,,	28th Dec.	,,	1
President Monroe	,,	28th April	,,	1
President Hoover	,,	10th Aug.	,,	1
Orville Wright	,,	19th Aug.	,,	1
Sven Hedin	,,	19th Feb.	,,	1
Chopin	,,	1st Mar.		1
William Dean Howells	,,	1st Mar.	,,	1
Bismarck	,,	1st April	,,	1

Sir Edwin Arnold	,,	10th June	,,	1
Sir Robert Ball	,,	1st July	,,	1
John Calvin	,,	10th July	,,	1
Mary Anderson	,,	28th July	,,	1
Alexandre Dumas	,,	28th July	,,	1
Oliver Wendell Holmes	,,	28th Aug.	,,	1
President Adams	,,	19th Oct.	,,	1
'Cheiro'	,,	1st Nov.	,,	1
Delcasse	,,	1st Nov.	,,	1
William Hogarth	,,	10th Nov.	,,	1
Captain Cook	,,	28th Oct.	,,	1
Danton	,,	28th Oct.	,,	1
Goethe	,,	28th Aug.	,,	1
Oliver Goldsmith	,,	10th Nov.	,,	1
Ferdinand de Lesseps	,,	19th Nov.	,,	1
Thomas More	,,	28th May	,,	1
Nansen	,,	10th Oct.	,,	1
Sir Charles Napier	,,	10th Aug.	,,	1
Charles Stewart Parnell	,,	28th June	,,	1
Adelina Patti	,,	10th Feb.	,,	1
Edgar Allan Poe	,,	19th Jan.	,,	1
Lord Russell of Killowen	,,	10th Nov.	,,	1
Sir H.M. Stanley	,,	28th Jan.	,,	1
Brigham Young	,,	1st June	,,	1
Brigitte Bardot	,,	28th Sept.	,,	1
Twiggy	,,	19th Sept.	,,	1
Richard Burton	,,	19th Nov.	,,	1
Charles Laughton	,,	1st July	,,	1

The Number 2

The number 2 stands in symbolism for the Moon. It has the feminine attributes of the Sun, and, for this reason alone, although number 1 and number 2 people are decidedly opposite in their characters their vibrations are harmonious and they make good combinations.

Number 2 persons are gentle by nature, imaginative, artistic, and romantic. Like the number 1 people, they are also inventive, but they are not as forceful in carrying out their ideas. Their qualities are more *on the mental* than the physical plane and they are seldom as strong physically as those born under the number 1.

Number 2 people are all those who are born on the 2nd, 11th, 20th, or 29th in any month, but their characteristics are the more marked if they are born between the 20th June and the 27th July, this period being what is called the 'House of the Moon.' 1 have added the seven days of the 'Cusp' to the 20th July.

Number 2 persons and number 1 vibrate together, and in a lesser degree with number 7 people, such as those born on the 7th, 16th, or 25th in any month.

Number 2 persons should endeavour to carry out their chief plans and ideas on days whose numbers vibrate with their own, such as on the 2nd, 11th, 20th, or 29th of any month, but more especially during the period of the 20th June to the 27th July.

The days of the week more fortunate or 'lucky' for them are Sunday, Monday, and Friday (the reason Friday is favourable in this case is that it is governed by Venus), and especially so if, like the number 1 people, one of their own numbers should fall on either of these days, such as the 2nd, 11th, 20th, or 29th, and next to these their interchangeable numbers of 1, 4, 7, such as the 1st, 4th, 7th, 10th, 13th, 16th, 19th, 22nd, 25th, 28th, or 31st.

The chief faults they should guard against are— being restless and unsettled, lack of continuity in their plans and ideas, and lack of self-confidence. They are also inclined to be oversensitive, and too easily get despondent and melancholy if they are not in happy surroundings.

For 'lucky' colours they should wear all shades of green, from the darkest to the lightest, also cream and white, but as far as possible they should avoid all dark colours, especially black, purple, and dark red.

Their 'lucky' stones and jewels are pearls, moonstones, pale green stones, and they should carry a piece of jade always with them, and, if possible, next their skin.

Famous People Born Under the Number 2

Thomas Chatterton, the Boy Poet	Born	20th Nov.	Represents 2
Swedenborg	,,	29th Jan	,, 2
Marie Antionette, Queen of France	,,	2nd Nov.	,, 2
Gladstone	,,	29th Dec.	,, 2
Queen Elizabeth of Rumania	,,	29th Dec.	,, 2
Sadi Carnot, President of France.	,,	11th Aug.	,, 2
General Boulanger	,,	29th April	,, 2
Napoleon III	,,	20th April	,, 2
King Victor Emmanuel III	,,	11th Nov.	,, 2
Edison	,,	11th Feb.	,, 2
David Garrick	,,	20th Feb.	,, 2
Lord Curzon of Kedleston	,,	11th Jan.	,, 2
Ibsen	,,	20th Mar.	,, 2
William Lecky	,,	20th Mar.	,, 2
Charles II	,,	29th May	,, 2

Sir Edward Elgar	Born	2nd June	Represents	2
Thomas Hardy	,,	2nd June	,,	2
Gluck	,,	2nd July	,,	2
President Adams	,,	11th July	,,	2
President Harding	,,	2nd Nov.	,,	2
President Poincare	,,	20th Aug.	,,	2
Paul Bourget	,,	2nd Sept.	,,	2
Henry George	,,	2nd Sept.	,,	2
Amelia E. Barr	,,	29th Mar.	,,	2
Max O'Rell	,,	2nd Mar.	,,	2
Eugene Field	,,	2nd Sept.	,,	2
Henry George	,,	2nd Sept.	,,	2
Joseph Jefferson	,,	20th Feb.	,,	2
Pope Leo XIII	,,	2nd Mar.	,,	2
Alfred de Musset	,,	11th Nov.	,,	2
Pope Pius X	,,	2nd June	,,	2
Bob Hope	,,	29th May	,,	2
Sophia Loren	,,	20th Sept.	,,	2
Bing Crosby	,,	2nd May	,,	2
Harold Wilson	,,	11th Mar.	,,	2

The Number 3

The number 3 stands in symbolism for the Planet Jupiter, a Planet which plays a most important role both in Astrology and in all systems of Numerology.

It is the beginning of what may be termed one of the main lines of force that runs right through all the numbers from 3 to 9.

It has a special relation to every third in the series, such as 3, 6, 9, and all their additions. These numbers added together in any direction produce a 9 as their final digit, and the 3, 6, 9, people are all sympathetic to one another.

Persons having a 3 for their Birth number are all

those who are born on the 3rd, 12th, 21st, or 30th, in any month, but the number 3 has still more significance if they should be born in what is called the 'period of the 3', from the 19th February to March 20th—27th, or from the 21st November to December 20th—27th.

Number 3 people, like the number 1 individuals, are decidedly ambitious; they are never satisfied by being in subordinate positions; their aim is to rise in the world, to have control and authority over others. They are excellent in the execution of commands; they love order and discipline in all things; they readily obey orders themselves, but they also insist on having their orders obeyed.

Number 3 people often rise to the very highest positions in any business, profession, or sphere in which they may be found. They often excel in positions of authority in the army and navy, in government, and in life generally; and especially in all posts of trust and responsibility, as they are extremely conscientious in carrying out their duties.

Their faults are that they are inclined to be dictatorial, to 'lay down the law' and to insist on carrying out their own ideas. For this reason, although they are not quarrelsome, they succeed in making many enemies.

Number 3 people are singularly proud; they dislike being under an obligation to others; they are also exceptionally independent, and chafe under the least restraint.

Number 3 people should endeavour to carry out their plans and aims on all days that vibrate to their own number, such as on the 3rd, 12th, 21st, and 30th of any month, but more especially when these dates fall in the 'period of the 3', such as from the 19th

February to March 20th—27th, and from the 21st November to December 20th—27th.

The days of the week more 'lucky' for them are Thursday, Friday and Tuesday; Thursday being the most important. These days are especially good if a number making a 3 should fall on it, such as the 3rd, 12th, 21st or 30th, and next in order their interchangeable numbers of 6 and 9 such as the 6th, 9th, 15th, 18th, 24th, 27th.

Number 3 people are more in harmony with those born under their own number or under the 6 and 9, such as all those who are born on a

3rd, 12th, 21st, 30th.
6th, 15th, 24th.
9th, 18th, 27th.

For 'lucky' colours they should wear some shade of mauve, violet, or purple, or some touch of these colours should always be with them; also in the rooms in which they live. All shades of blue, crimson, and rose are also favourable to them, but more as secondary colours.

Their 'lucky' stone is the amethyst. They should always have one on their persons, and, if possible, wear it next their skin.

Famous People Born Under the Number 3

King George V	Born	3rd June	Represents	3
Emperor Frederick of Germany	,,	21st Nov.	,	3
Gambetta of Italy	,,	30th Oct.	,,	3
Lord Russel	,,	12th Aug.	,,	3
Abraham Lincoln, President	,,	12th Feb.	,,	3
Winston Churchill, M.P.	,,	30th Nov.	,,	3

Field-Marshal Lord Roberts V.C.	,,	30th Sept.	,,	3
Rudyard Kipling	,,	30th Dec.	,,	3
Sir Arthur Sullivan	,,	12th May	,,	3
Sir Charles Hawtrey	,,	21st Sept.	,,	3
Lord Beaconsfield	,,	21st Dec.	,,	3
Darwin	,,	12th Feb.	,,	3
George Pullman	,,	3rd Mar.	,,	3
Bishop Heber	,,	21st April	,,	3
Sir Alfred Austin	,,	30th May	,,	3
Richard Cobden	,,	3rd June	,,	3
The Earl of Aberdeen	,,	3rd Aug.	,,	3
King Haakon	,,	3rd Aug.	,,	3
George IV	,,	12th Aug.	,,	3
The First Lord Oxford and Asquith	,,	12th Sept.	,,	3
William Cullen Bryant	,,	3rd Nov.	,,	3
Mrs. Craigie	,,	3rd Nov.	,,	3
Pope Benedict	,,	21st Nov.	,,	3
'Mark Twain'	,,	30th Nov	,,	3
President Felix Faure	,,	30th Jan..	,,	3
Mendelssohn	,,	3rd Feb.	,,	3
Cardinal Newman	,,	21st Feb..	,,	3
Dean Swift	,,	30th Nov.	,,	3
Voltaire	,,	21st Nov.	,,	3
Ramsay Mac Donald	,,	12th Oct..	,,	3
Joseph Stalin	,,	21st Dec..	,,	3
Frank Sinatra	,,	12th Dec.	,,	3
John Osborn	,,	12th Dec.	,,	3
Henry Moore	,,	30th July	,,	3

The Number 4

The number 4 stands in its symbolism for the Planet

Uranus. It is considered related to the Sun, number 1, and in occultism is written as 4—1.

Number 4 people have a distinct character of their own. They appear to view everything from an opposite angle to everyone else. In an argument they will always take the opposite side, and although not meaning to be quarrelsome, yet they bring about opposition and make a great number of secret enemies who constantly work against them.

They seem quite naturally to take a different view of anything that is presented to their minds. They instinctively rebel against rules and regulations, and if they can have their way they reverse the order of things, even in communities and governments. They often rebel against constitutional authority and set up new rules and regulations either in domestic or public life. They are inclined to be attracted to social questions and reforms of all kinds, and are very positive and unconventional in their views and opinions.

Number 4 people are all those who are born on the 4th, 13th, 22nd, and 31st in any month; their individuality is still more pronounced if they are born in the Zodiacal period of the Sun and Moon, namely, between the 21st June and July 20th—27th (Moon period) and from the 21st July to the end of August (Sun period).

Number 4 people do not make friends easily. They seem more attracted to persons born under the 1, 2, 7, and 8 numbers.

They are seldom as successful in worldly or material matters as people born under the other numbers, and as a rule they are more or less indifferent as to the accumulation of wealth. If they do acquire money or have it given to them they generally surprise people by the way they employ it or the use they put it to.

They should endeavour to carry out their plans and ideas on all days that have their number 4, such as the 4th, 13th, 22nd, and 31st of any month, but especially so if these dates come in their strong period, from the 21st June to July 20th—27th, or from the 22nd July to the end of August.

The days of the week more fortunate or 'lucky' for them are Saturday, Sunday, and Monday, especially so if their 'own number' should fall on one of these days, such as the 4th, 13th, 22nd, or 31st, and next in order their interchangeable numbers of 1, 2, 7, such as the 1st, 2nd, 7th, 10th, 11th, 16th, 19th, 20th, 25th, 28th, or 29th.

The chief faults are that they are most highly strung and sensitive, very easily wounded in their feelings, inclined to feel lonely and isolated, and are likely to become despondent and melancholy unless they have achieved success. As a rule they make few real friends, but to the few they have, they are most devoted and loyal, but are always inclined to take the part of 'the under-dog' in any argument or any cause they espouse.

For 'lucky' colours, they should wear what are called 'half-shades,' 'half-tones,' or 'electric colours.' 'Electric blues' and greys seem to suit them best of all.

Their 'lucky' stone is the sapphire, light or dark, and if possible they should wear this stone next their skin.

Famous People Born Under the Number 4

The Earl of Stafford	Born	13th April	Represents 4
George Washington	,,	22nd Feb.	,, 4
Lord Byron	,,	22nd Jan.	,, 4
George Eliot	,,	22nd Nov.	,, 4

Lord Baden-Powell of Gilwell	,,	22nd Feb.	,,	4
The Queen of Holland	,,	31st Aug.	,,	4
Sarah Bernhardt	,,	22nd Oct.	,,	4
Thomas Carlyle	,,	4th Dec.	,,	4
Faraday	,,	22nd Oct.	,,	4
Lord Leighton	,,	4th Dec.	,,	4
Prince Charlie	,,	31st Dec.	,,	4
Sir Francis Bacon	,,	22nd Jan.	,,	4
James Russell Lowell	,,	22nd Feb.	,,	4
Haydn	,,	31st April	,,	4
Thomas Huxley	,,	4th May	,,	4
Alphonse Daudet	,,	13th May	,,	4
Sir Arthur Conan Doyle	,,	22nd May	,,	4
George III	,,	4th June	,,	4
Julian Hawthone	,,	22nd June	,,	4
Rider Haggard	,,	22nd June	,,	4
General Goettals	,,	22nd June	,,	4
Nathaniel Hawthorne	,,	4th July	,,	4
Emma Eames	,,	13th Aug.	,,	4
Archbishop Corrigan	,,	13th Aug.	,,	4
Ex-Sultan Abdul Hamid	,,	22nd Sept.	,,	4
Saint Augustine	,,	13th Nov.	,,	4
Heinrich Heine	,,	13th Dec.	,,	4
Immanuel Kant	,,	22nd April	,,	4
Sir Isaac Pitman	,,	4th Jan.	,,	4
Pope Pius IX	,,	13th May	,,	4
Russell Sage	,,	4th Aug.	,,	4
Schubert	,,	31st Jan.	,,	4
Sir Arthur Sullivan	,,	13th May	,,	4
Richard Wagner	,,	22nd May	,,	4
Sir Hamilton Harty	,,	4th Dec.	,,	4
Laurence Olivier	,,	22nd May	,,	4
Maria Callas	,,	4th Dec.	,,	4

Charles de Gaulle	,,	22nd Nov.	,,	4
Yehudi Menuhin	,,	22nd April	,,	4

The Number 5

The number 5 stands in symbolism for the Planet Mercury, and is versatile and mercurial in all its characteristics.

Number 5 people are all those who are born on the 5th, 14th, and 23rd in any month, but their characteristics are still more marked if they are born in what is called the 'period of the 5,' which is from the 21st May to June 20th—27th, and from the 21st August to September 20th—27th.

Number 5 people *make friends easily* and get on with persons born under *almost any other number*, but their best friends are those who are born under their own number, such as the 5th, 14th, and 23rd of any month.

Number 5 people are mentally very highly strung. They live on their nerves and appear to crave excitement.

They are quick in thought and decisions, and impulsive in their actions. They detest any plodding kind of work and seem naturally to drift into all methods of making money quickly. They have a keen sense of making money by inventions and new ideas. They are born speculators, prone to Stock Exchange transactions, and generally are willing and ready to run risks in all they undertake.

They have the most wonderful elasticity of character. They rebound quickly from the heaviest blow; nothing seems to affect them for very long; like their symbol, quicksilver, which Mercury represents, the blows of Fate leave no indentations on their character. If they are by nature good they remain so; if bad, not all the preaching in the world will have the slightest effect on them.

Number 5 people should endeavour to carry out their plans and aims on all days that fall under their 'own number,' such as the 5th, 14th, or 23rd of any month, but more especially when these dates fall in the 'period of the 5,' namely from the 21st May to June 20th—27th, or from the 21st August to September 20th—27th.

The days of the week more fortunate or 'lucky' for them are Wednesday and Friday, especially if their 'own number' falls on one of these days.

Their greatest drawback is that they exhaust their nervous strength to such an extent that they often fall victims to nervous breakdowns of the worst kind, and under any mental tension they easily become irritable and quick-tempered, unable to 'suffer fools gladly.'

Their 'lucky' colours are all shades of light grey, white, and glistening materials, but just as they can make friends with people born under all kinds of numbers, so can they wear all shades of colours, but by far the best for them are light shades, and they should wear dark colours as rarely as possible.

Their 'lucky' stone is the diamond, and all glittering or shimmering things; also ornaments made of platinum or silver, and if possible, they should wear a diamond set in platinum next their skin.

Famous People Born Under the Number 5

St. Louis of France	Born	23rd May	Represents 5
Louis XVI	,,	23rd Aug.	,, 5
Empress Eugenie	,,	5th May	,, 5
H.M. King George VI	,,	14th Dec.	,, 5

H.R.H. The Duke of Windsor	,,	23rd June	,,	5
Samuel Pepys	,,	23rd Feb.	,,	5
Sir Hiram Maxim	,,	5th Feb.	..	5
Lord Lister	,,	3rd April	,,	5
T.P. O'Connor, M.P.	,,	5th Oct.	.,	5
Jean de Reske	,,	14th Jan.	,,	5
Sir Henry Bessemer	,,	14th Mar.	,,	5
Humbert I of Italy	,,	14th Mar.	,,	5
Shakespeare	,,	23rd April	.,	5
Thomas Hood	,.	23rd May	..	5
Chateaubriand	,,	14th Sept.	.,	5
Benedict Arnold	.,	14th Jan.	.,	5
Barnum	,,	5th July	.,	5
Erard	,,	5th April	,,	5
Handel	,,	23rd Feb.	,,	5
Fahrenheit	,,	14th May	.,	5
Josephine, Queen of France	,,	23rd June	,,	5
Karl Marx	,,	5th May	,,	5
Mesmer	,,	23rd May	.,	5
Sir Gilbert Parker	,,	23rd Nov.	,,	5
Cardinal Richelieu	,,	5th Sept.	,,	5
W.T. Stead	,,	5th Feb.	,,	5
Talleyrand	,,	14th Feb.	,,	5
Neil Armstrong	,,	5th Aug.	,,	5
Dwight Eisenhower	,,	14th Oct.	,,	5
Albert Einstein	,,	14th Mar.	,,	5

The Number 6

The number 6 stands in symbolism for the Planet Venus. Persons having a 6 as their Birth number are all those who are born on the 6th, 15th, or 24th, of any month, but they are more especially influenced by this number if they are born in what is called the 'House of the 6th' which is from the 20th April to May 20th—27th, and from the 21st September to October 20th—27th.

As a rule all number 6 people are extremely magnetic; they attract others to them, and they are loved and often worshipped by those under them.

They are very determined in carrying out their plans, and may, in fact, be deemed obstinate and unyielding, except when they themselves become deeply attached: in such a case they become devoted slaves to those they love.

Although number 6 people are considered influenced by the Planet Venus, yet as a rule theirs is more the 'mother love' than the sensual. They lean to the romantic and ideal in all matters of the affections. In some ways they take very strongly after the supposed qualities of Venus, in that they love beautiful things, they make most artistic homes, are fond of rich colours, also paintings, statuary, and music.

If rich they are most generous to art and artists, they love to entertain their friends and make everyone happy about them, but the one thing they cannot stand is discord and jealousy.

When roused by anger they will brook no opposition, and will fight to the death for whatever person or cause they espouse, or out of their sense of duty.

The number 6 people have got the power of making more friends than any other class, with the exception of the number 5, but especially so with all persons born under the vibration of the 3, the 6, the 9, or all their series.

Their most important days in the week are Tuesdays, Thursdays, and Fridays, and especially so if a number of 3, 6, or 9, such as the 3rd, 6th, 9th, 12th, 18th, 21st, 24th, 27th, or 30th, should fall on one of those days.

Number 6 people should endeavour to carry out their plans and aims on all dates that fall under their 'own number,' such as the 6th, 15th, or 24th, of any month, but more especially when these dates fall in the 'period of the 6,' namely, between the 20th April and May 20th—27th, or from the 21st September to October 20th—2th.

Their 'lucky' colours are all shades of blue, from the lightest to the darkest, also all shades of rose or pink, but they should avoid wearing black or dark purple.

Their 'lucky' stone is especially the turquoise, and, as far as possible, they should wear one, or a piece of turquoise matrix, next their skin. Emeralds are also 'lucky' for the number 6 people.

Famous People Born Under the Number 6

Queen Victoria	Born	24th May	Represents	6
Napoleon I	,,	15th Aug.	,,	6
Frederick the Great	,,	24th Jan.	,,	6
Duke of Marlborough	,,	24th May	,,	6
Emperor Maximilian of Mexico	,,	6th July	,,	6
Henry VI	,,	6th Dec.	,,	6
Oliver Cromwell	,,	24th April	,,	6
Cecil Rhodes	,,	6th July	,,	6
Joan of Arc	,,	6th Jan.	,,	6
Admiral Lord Jellicoe	,,	6th Dec.	,,	6
President Taft	,,	15th Sept.	,,	6
Sir Walter Scott	,,	6th Dec.	,,	6
Sir Henry Irving	,,	6th Feb.	,,	6
Joseph Choate	,,	24th Jan.	,,	6
Susan B. Anthony	,,	15th Feb.	,,	6
Michelangelo	,,	6th Mar.	,,	6

Elizabeth Browning	,,	6th Mar.	,,	6
Henry Ward Beecher	,,	24th June	,,	6
President Diaz	,,	15th Sept.	,,	6
Sir William Herschel	..	15th Nov.	,,	6
Grace Darling	..	24th Nov.	,,	6
Warren Hastings	..	6th Dec.	,,	6
King George I	,.	24th Dec.	,,	6
John Knox	..	24th Nov.	,,	6
Moliere	,,	15th Jan.	,,	6
Max Muller	..	6th Dec.	.,	6
Daniel O'Connell	..	6th Aug.	.,	6
Count de Paris	,,	24th Aug.	,,	6
Admiral Peary	,,	6th May	,,	6
Sir Arthur Pinero	,,	24th May	,,	6
Rembrandt	,,	15th July	.,	6
Alfred Tennyson	,,	6th Aug.	,,	6
George Westinghouse	,,	6th Oct.	;,	6
P.G. Wodehouse	.,	15th Oct.	.,	6
Gamal Nasser	,,	15th Jan.	,	6
Alexander Fleming	,,	6th Aug.	,,	6

The Number 7

The number 7 stands in symbolism for the Planet Neptune, and represents all persons born under the 7, namely those who are born on the 7th, 16th, or 25th of any month, but more especially influences such persons if they were born from the 21st June to July 20th—27th, the period of the Zodiac called the 'House of the Moon.' The Planet Neptune has always been considered as associated with the Moon, and, as the part of the Zodiac I have mentioned is also called the First House of Water, the connection of Neptune whose very name is always associated with Water is then logical and easily understood.

Now, as the number of the Moon is always given

as a 2, this explains why it is that the number 7 people have as their secondary number the 2, and get on well and make friends easily with all those born under the Moon numbers, namely, the 2nd, 11th, 20th, and 29th. of any month, especially so if they are also born in the 'House of the Moon,' from the 21st of June to the end of July.

People born under the number 7, namely, on the 7th, 16th, or 25th of any month, are very independent, original, and have strongly marked individuality.

At heart they love change and travel, being restless in their natures. If they have the means of gratifying their desires they visit foreign countries and become keenly interested in the affairs of far-off lands. They devour books on travel and have a wide universal knowledge of the world at large.

They often make extremely good writers, painters, or poets, but in everything they do, they sooner or later show a peculiar philosophical outlook on life that tinges all their work.

As a class they care little about the material things of life; they often become rich by their original ideas or methods of business, but if they do they are just as likely to make large donations from their wealth to charities or institutions. The women of this number generally marry well, as they are always anxious about the future, and feel that they need some rock to rest on lest the waters of Fate sweep them away.

The number 7 people have good ideas about business, or rather their plans are good if they will only carry them out. They have usually a keen desire to travel and read a great deal about far-off countries. If they can they will become interested in matters concerning the sea, and in trade or business they often become merchants, exporters, and importers, dealing with foreign countries, and owners or captains of ships if they can get chance.

Number 7 people have very peculiar ideas about religion. They dislike following the beaten track; they create a religion of their own, but one that appeals to the imagination and based on the mysterious.

These people usually have remarkable dreams and a great leaning to occultism; they have the gift of intuition, clairvoyance, and a peculiar quieting magnetism of their own that has great influence over others.

Number 7 people should endeavour to carry out their plans and aims on all days that fall under their 'own number,' such as the 7th, 16th, or 25th of any month, but more especially when these dates fall in the 'period of the 7,' namely, from the 21st June to July 20th—27th and less strongly from that date to the end of August.

The days of week more fortunate of 'lucky' for them are the same as for the number 2 people, namely, Sunday and Monday, especially if their 'own number' falls on one of these days, or their interchangeable numbers of 1, 2, 4, such as the 1st, 2nd, 4th, 10th, 11th, 13th, 19th, 20th, 22nd, 28th, 29th, or 31st.

Their 'lucky' colours are all shades of green, pale shades, also white and yellow, and they should avoid all heavy dark colours as much as possible.

Their 'lucky' stones are moonstones, 'cat's-eyes,' and pearls, and if possible, they should wear a moonstone or a piece of moss next their skin.

Famous People Born Under the Number 7

Queen Elizabeth I	Born	7th Sept.	Represents 7
Louis XIV	,,	16th Sept.	,, 7

Empress Charlotte of Mexico	,,	7th June	,,	7
Lord Rosebery	,,	7th May	,,	7
Lord Balfour	,,	25th July	,,	7
Admiral Earl Beatty	,,	16th Jan.	,,	7
Bonar Law, M.P.	,,	16th Sept.	,,	7
Charles Dickens	,,	7th Feb.	,,	7
Sir Joshua Reynolds	,,	16th July	,,	7
Oscar Wilde	,,	16th Oct.	,,	7
Ernst Haeckel	,,	16th Feb.	,,	7
Camille Flammarion	,,	25th Feb.	,,	7
Prince Imperial	,,	16th Mar.	,,	7
Sir John Franklin	,,	16th April	,,	7
Robert Browning	,,	7th May	,,	7
Ralph Waldo Emerson	,,	25th June	,,	7
Dean Farrar	,,	7th Aug.	,,	7
Bret Harte	,,	25th Aug.	,,	7
Philip D. Armour	,,	16th May	,,	7
Andrew Carnegie	,,	25th Nov.	,,	7
Sir Isaac Newton	,,	25th Dec.	,,	7
Rousseau	,,	16th April	,,	7
Sardou	,,	7th Sept.	,,	7
De Witt Talmage	,,	7th Jan	,,	7
William Wordsworth	,,	7th April	,,	7
Noel Coward	,,	16th Dec.	,,	7
David Frost	,,	7th April	,,	7
Pablo Picasso	,,	25th Oct.	,,	7
Billy Graham	,,	7th Nov.	,,	7

The Number 8

The number 8 stands in symbolism for the Planet Saturn. This number influences all persons born on the 8th, 17th, or 26th in any month, but still more so if their birthday comes between the 21st December and the 26th January, which period is called the House of

Saturn (Positive), and from the 26th January to February 19—26th, the period called the House of Saturn (Negative).

These people are invariably much misunderstood in their lives, and perhaps for this reason they feel intensely lonely at heart.

They have deep and very intense natures, great strength of individuality; they generally play some important role on life's stage, but usually one which is fatalistic, or as the instrument of Fate for others.

If at all religious they go to extremes and are fanatics in their zeal. In any cause they take up, they attempt to carry it through in spite of all arguments or opposition, and in doing so they generally make bitter and relentless enemies.

They often appear cold and undemonstrative, though in reality they have warm hearts towards the oppressed of all classes; but they hide their feelings and allow people to think just what they please.

These number 8 people are either great successes or great failures; there appears to be no happy medium in their case.

If ambitious, they generally aim for public life or government responsibility of some kind, and often hold very high positions involving great sacrifice on their part.

It is not, however, from a worldly standpoint, a fortunate number to be born under, and such persons often are called on to face the very greatest sorrows, losses, and humiliations.

The 'lucky' colours for people born under the 8 are all shades of dark grey, black, dark blue, and purple. If number 8 persons were to dress in light colours they would look awkward, and as if there were something wrong with them.

The number 8 being a Saturn number, Saturday is therefore their most important day, but on account of the number 4 having influence on a Sunday and in a secondary way on a Monday, the number 8 people will find Saturday, Sunday, and Monday their most important days.

Number 8 people should endeavour to carry out their plans and aims on all days that fall under their 'own number', such as the 8th, 17th, or 26th in any month, but more especially so when these dates fall in the 'period of the 8', namely, from the 21st December to January 20th—27th, and from that date to February 19th—26th; also if these dates fall on a Saturday, Sunday, or Monday, or their interchangeable number, which is 4, such as the 4th, 13th, 22nd, or 31st.

Their 'lucky' stones are the amethyst and the dark toned sapphire, also the black pearl or the black diamond and if possible they should wear one of these next their skin.

The number 8 is a difficult number to explain. It represents two worlds, the material and the spiritual. It is in fact, if one regards it, like two circles just touching together.

It is composed of two equal numbers: 4 and 4.

From the earliest ages it has been associated with the symbol of an irrevocable Fate, both in connection with the lives of individuals or nations. In Astrology it stands for Saturn, which is also called the Planet of Fate.

One side of the nature of this number represents upheaval, revolution, anarchy, waywardness, and eccentricities of all kinds.

The other side represents philosophic thought, a strong leaning towards occult studies, religious devotion, concentration of purpose, zeal for any cause espoused, and a fatalistic outlook colouring all actions.

All persons who have the number 8 clearly associated with their lives feel that they are distinct and different from their fellows. At heart they are lonely; they are misunderstood, and they seldom reap the reward for the good they may do while they are living. After their death they are often extolled, their works praised, and lasting tributes offered to their memory.

Those on the lower plane generally come into conflict with human justice and have some tragic ending to their lives. Those on the higher plane carry their misunderstood motives and lay bare the tragedy of their souls before Divine Justice.

To distinguish in which of these two classes a number 8 person falls, one must find by the comparison of their 'fadic' numbers if they are completely dominated by the recurrence of 8 in the principal events of their lives, or if some other equally powerfull number such as the 1, 3, or 6 series does not more or less balance the sequel of events registered under the 8 and all its series.

If the latter is the case, one may be sure that by the long series of reincarnations they have passed through, they have paid the price in some former state, and are now passing towards the higher, where Divine Justice will give them their reward.

If, on the contrary, we find that the person is completely dominated by the number 8, always recurring in important events, or if instead of 8 the nearly equally fatalistic number of 4 is continually recurring, we may then be sure that we are in the presence of one of those strange playthings of Fate with the possibilities that tragedy may be interwoven in their Destiny.

In the more ordinary tragedies of everday life, we can find an illuminating example in the life and execution of Crippen, whose principal actions were singularly influenced by the terrible combination of the 8 and the 4.

Looking back over his career, and especially the events which led up to his paying that terrible forfeit at the hands of the law, one will find these numbers associated in the most dramatic way with this man's life, as illustrated by the following facts:

The figures of the year he was born in (1862), if added together, produce an 8 (17 equals 1 plus 7 equals 8). He was born on the 26th January, or 2 plus 6 equals 8.

His wife was not seen alive after dinner with him on the 31st January, which is a 4, and the month of January is itself called the House of Saturn, whose number is an 8.

He made his statement to Inspector Drew (which was later to be used as overwhelming evidence against him) on the 8th July.

The human remains were found in the cellar on 13th July, which again makes the number 4.

To try to escape he chose the name 'Robinson', which has, strange to say, 8 letters in it.

He was recognised on board the *Montrose* on the 22nd July, which again equals a 4.

The name of the ship he chose to leave Europe by (the *Montrose*) has 8 letters, and the ship that brought him back to his doom, the *Megantic*, was also composed of 8 letters.

He was arrested, as this ship reached Canada, on the morning of the 31st July, which again equals 4.

His trial finished on Saturday, 22nd October, which is again the 4, and October being the month of 'the detriment of Saturn' gives again the 8.

The occult number by which Saturday is designated is an 8.

His execution was fixed for the 8th November.

His appeal was heard and refused on Saturday, 5th November. The 5 added to the 8, which Saturday is a symbol of, again makes the figure 13, which number again equals a 4.

When his appeal failed, the date of execution was changed to the 23rd November. The addition of 2—3 makes a 5, and the division of Zodiac which represents this portion of November is designated as 3; and this 3, if added to the date (the 23rd), makes the figure 26, which by addition (2 plus 6) again equals 8. Or if the 3 were added to the number of 23 we would get 26 or the 8.

The symbol of the number 8, I may also mention, from time immemorial, in occult studies, is called the 'symbol of human justice.'

Lastly, *when Crippen's 'Key numbers,' the 4 and 8, came together, it was the fatal year of his life. He was 48 years old when executed.*

It is not my province to judge or condemn this unfortunate being. Crippen, in any case, suffered as few men have been called upon to suffer; but I may add that the combination of such numbers as 4 and 8 as the 'Key numbers' in any life, indicate an individual terribly under the influence of Fate, and one especially unfortunate through his or her affections.

I have followed out many cases of people having similar 'Key numbers,' and in every case they seem sooner or later to come into conflict with what the 8 represents, namely, the symbol of 'human justice.' They are generally condemned, even in ordinary social life, by the weight of circumstantial evidence, and they usually die with their secret, appealing, as it were, from the sentence of 'human justice,' which, as a rule, has been against them, to that of the Divine Justice in the world beyond.

The occult symbol of 8 has from time immemorial been represented by the figure of Justice with a Sword pointing upwards and a Balance or Scales in the left hand.

There are many very curious things in history as regards this number. The Greeks called it the number of Justice on account of its equal divisions of equally even numbers.

The Jews practised circumcision on the 8th day after birth. At their Feast of Dedication they kept 8 candles burning, and this Feast lasted 8 days.

Eight prophets were descended from Rahab.

There were 8 sects of Pharisees.

Noah was the 8th direct descent from Adam.

The strange number of three eights (888) is considered by students of Occultism to be the number of Jesus Christ in His aspect as the Redeemer of the world. Curiously enough, the addition of 888 makes 24 and 2 plus 4 gives the 6 which is the number of Venus, the representative of Love.

This number 888 given to Christ is in direct opposition to 666 which Revelation says 'is the number of the Beast or the number of Man.' The numbers 666 if added together give 18 (1 plus 8 equals 9). This 9 is the number of Mars, the symbol of War, destruction, and force, which is decidedly the opposition of the 6 with the symbol of Love.

Remarkable People Born Under the 8

Mary I of England	Born	17th Feb. Represents	8
King Albert of Belgium	,,	8th April	,,	8
Queen Mary	,,	26th May	,,	8
Alfonso XIII of Spain	,,	17th May	,,	8
Joseph Chamberlain	,,	8th July	,,	8
George Bernard Shaw	,,	26th July	,,	8
David Lloyd George	,,	17th Jan.	,,	8
Prince Albert	,,	26th Aug.	,,	8
Admiral Dewey	,,	26th Dec.	,,	8
Bernadotte, King of Sweden	,,	26th Jan.	,,	8
Colonel Cody	,,	26th Feb.	,,	8
Wilkie Collins	,,	8th Jan.	,,	8
Louis Conde of France	,,	8th Sept.	,,	8
Sir Humphry Davy	,,	17th Dec.	,,	8
Gounod	,,	17th June	,,	8
Jenner	,,	17th May	,,	8
La Fontaine	,,	8th July	,,	8
Mary, Queen of Scots	,,	8th Dec.	,,	8
Sir John Millais	,,	8th June	,,	8
General von Moltke	,,	26th Oct.	,,	8
Pierpont-Morgan	,,	117th April	,,	8
Richard I	,,	8th Sept.	,,	8
J.D. Rockefeller	,,	8th July	,,	8
Jules Verne	,,	8th Feb.	,,	8
John Wesley	,,	17th June	,,	8
Christiaan Barnard	,,	8th Oct.	,,	8
Elizabeth Taylor	,,	17th Feb.	,,	8
Rudolf Nureyev	,,	17th Mar.	,,	8
Compton Mackenzie	,,	17th Jan.	,,	8

The Number 9

The number 9 stands in symbolism for the Planet Mars. This number influences all persons born on the

9th, 18th, and 27th of any month, but still more so if their birthday falls in the period between the 21st March and April 19th—26th (called the House of Mars Positive) or in the period between the 21st October and November 20th—27th (called the House of Mars Negative).

Number 9 persons are fighters in all they attempt in life. They usually have difficult times in their early years, but generally they are, in the end, successful by their grit, strong will, and determination.

In character, they are hasty in temper, impulsive, independent, and desire to be their own masters.

When the number 9 is noticed to be more than usually dominant in the dates and events of their lives they will be found to make great enemies, to cause strife and opposition wherever they may be, and they are often wounded or killed either in warfare or in the battle of life.

They have great courage and make excellent soldiers or leaders in any cause they espouse.

Their greatest dangers arise from foolhardiness and impulsiveness in word and action. They are also peculiarly prone to accidents from fire and explosions and rarely get through life without injury from such causes. As a general rule they go under many operations by the surgeon's knife.

They usually experience many quarrels and strife in their home life, either with their own relations or with the family they marry into.

They strongly resent criticism, and even when not conceited, they have always a good opinion of themselves, brooking no interference with their plans. They like to be 'looked up to' and recognised as 'the head of the house.'

They are resourceful and excellent in organisation,

but they must have the fullest control; if not, they lose heart and stand aside and let things go to pieces.

For affection and sympathy they will do almost anything, and the men of this number can be made the greatest fools of, if some clever woman gets pulling at their heartstrings.

As a rule they get on with persons whose birth date is one of the series of 3, 6, or 9, such as those born on the 3rd, 6th, 9th, 12th, 15th, 18th, 21st, 24th, 27th, or 30th of any month. All these numbers are in harmonious vibration to the number 9 people.

This number 9 has some very curious properties. It is the only number in calculation that, multiplied by any number, always reproduces itself, as for example 9 times 2 is 18, and 8 plus 1 becomes again the 9. and so on *with every number it is multiplied by*.

It is, perhaps, not uninteresting to notice that:

At the 9th day the ancients buried their dead.

At the 9th hour Christ died on the Cross.

The Romans held a feast in memory of their dead every 9th year.

In some of the Hebrew writings it is taught that God has 9 times descended to this earth:

1st in the Garden of Eden,

2nd at the confusion of tongues at Babel,

3rd at the destruction of Sodom and Gomorrah,

4th to Moses at Horeb,

5th at Sinai when the Ten Commandments were given,

6th to Balaam,

7th to Elisha,

8th in the Tabernacle,

9th in the Temple at Jerusalem,

and it is taught that at the 10th coming this earth

will pass away and a new one will be created.

Both the First and Second Temples of the Jews were destroyed on the 9th day of the Jewish month called Ab. On the 9th day of Ab Jews who follow their religion cannot wear the Talith and Phylacteries until the Sun has set.

There are so many curious things connected with the number 9 that it would not be possible to deal with one-half of them in a book of this description.

This number is supposed to be a fortunate one to be born under, provided one controls it and is not carried away by the excesses of temper and violence that it also represents.

The 'lucky' colours for persons born under the number 9 are all shades of crimson or red, also all rose tones and pink.

Their most important days in the week are Tuesday, Thursday, and Friday, but more especially Tuesday (called Mars Day).

Number 9 people should endeavour to carry out their plans and aims on all days that fall under their 'own number', such as the 9th, 18th, or 27th in any month, but more especially when these dates fall in the 'period of the 9,' between the 21st March and April 19th—26th, or from the 21st October to November 20th—27th. And when the 9th, 18th, or 27th falls on their 'own day', as mentioned above, or one of their interchangeable numbers which are the 3 and 6, such as the 3rd, 6th, 12th, 15th, 21st, 24th, and 30th.

Their 'lucky' stones are the ruby, garnet, and bloodstone, and they should wear one of these stones next their skin.

For all purposes of occult calculation the numbers 7 and 9 are considered the most important of all.

The 7 has always been understood to relate to the spiritual plane, acting as the God or creative force on the Earth, and being creative, it is the uplifting 'urge' towards the higher development of the spiritual in humanity.

The 9 on the contrary, being, in the Planetary World, the representative of the Planet Mars, is the number of physical force in every form, and consequently stands in relation to the material.

When this explanation is carefully considered it throws an illuminating light on that mysterious text in Revelation, chapter xiii, verse 18: 'Here is wisdom. Let him that hath understanding count the number of the beast, for it is the number of man, and his number is 666'.

This strange text has puzzled the theological mind for centuries, yet if you will take the trouble to add 666 together you will get 18, and 1 plus 8 gives you the figure 9, which in turn represents the 9 Planets of our Solar System, the 9 numbers upon which man builds all his calculations, and beyond which he cannot go except by continual repetition of the numbers 1 to 9.

'666' producing its 'spirit number' (as explained in a preceding page) of 9 is therefore, in all truth as Revelation states, 'the number of man.'

The hidden meaning of this number is one of the greatest secrets of occultism, and has been concealed in a thousand ways, just as the cryptic text in Revelation has hidden it for centuries from the minds of theologians.

The number 9 representing man and everything to do with the physical and material plane, is the number of force, energy, destruction, and war in its most dominant quality. In its relation to ordinary life it denotes energy, ambition, leadership, dominion. It represents iron, the metal from which the weapons of warfare are made, and the Planet Mars which it stands for in Astrology is the Ruler of the Zodiacal Sign Aries which is the Sign of the Zodiac which governs England. This symbolism was evidently well known by Shakespeare when he wrote, 'England, thou seat of Mars.'

The number 9 is an emblem of matter that can never be destroyed, so the number 9 when multiplied by any number always reproduces itself, no matter what the extent of the number is that has been employed.

The Novendiale was a fast in the Roman Catholic Church to avert calamities, and from this came the Roman Catholic system of Neuvaines.

In Freemasonry there is an order of 'Nine Elected Knights, and in the working of this Order 9 roses, 9 lights, and 9 knocks must be used.

All ancient races encouraged a fear of the number 9, and all its multiples.

The number 9 is considered a fortunate number to be born under, provided the man or woman does not ask for a peaceful or monotonous life, and can control their nature in not making enemies.

Remarkable People Born Under the 9

Kaiser Wilhelm	Born	27th Jan. Represents	9
King Edward VII	,,	9th Nov. ,,	9
Sir Evelyn Wood, V.C.	,,	9th Feb. ,,	9
President Theodore Roosevelt	,,	27th Oct. ,,	9
President Grover Cleveland	,,	18th Mar. ,,	9

Lord Carson	,,	9th Feb.	,,	9
Sam Gompers	,,	27th Jan.	,,	9
Ernest Renan	,,	27th Feb.	,,	9
President Ulysses Grant	,,	27th April	,,	9
Sir James Barrie	,,	9th May	,,	9
Julia Ward Howe	,,	27th May	,,	9
Jay Gould	,,	27th May	,,	9
Elizabeth, Empress of Austria	,,	18th Aug.	,,	9
Franz Josef, Emperor of Austria	,,	18th Aug.	,,	9
Fredrick III of Germany	,,	19th Oct.	,,	9
Kepler	,,	27th Dec.	,,	9
Louis Kossuth	,,	27th April	,,	9
Leopold II, of Belgium	,,	9th April	,,	9
Nicholas II, of Russia	,,	18th May	,,	9
Paganini	,,	18th Feb.	,,	9
Whitelaw Reid	,,	27th Oct.	,,	9
George Stephenson	,,	9th June	,,	9
Edward Heath	,,	9th July	,,	9
Richard Nixon	,,	9th Jan.	,,	9
Margot Fonteyn	,,	18th May	,,	9
Marlene Dietrich	,,	27th Dec.	,,	9
Greta Garbo	,,	18th Sept.	,,	9
Peter Sellers	,,	18th Sept.	,,	9

3

The Occult Symbolism of 'Compound' Numbers with Illustrations

I AM NOW GOING to put before my readers one of the most amazing systems comprised in the occult calculations of names and numbers that it has been my good fortune to elucidate. This system, which has never before been made public on the lines I am going to present it, will, I know, be of inestimable value to those who may care to follow the rules I shall give.

I feel sure, from long experience, that the occult philosophy I am now about to pass on will be of the greatest *practical utility* to every man or woman, who wishes for aid in the hard struggle for existence that is, alas, the fate of so many sons and daughters of humanity.

Shakespeare, that Prince of Philosophers, whose thoughts will adorn English literature for all time, laid down the well-known axiom: 'There is a tide in the affairs of men which, taken at the flood, leads on to fortune.' The question has been asked again and again: Is there some means of knowing when the moment has come *to take the tide at the flood*?

My answer to this question is, that the great Architect of the Universe in His Infinite Wisdom so created all things in such harmony of design that He endowed the human mind with some part of that omnipotent knowledge which is the attribute of the Divine Mind as the Creator of all.

It is this desire for knowledge implanted in the mind of humanity that places mankind above the animal creation, and makes men and women as 'gods' in their desire 'to know'.

We are told that Solomon the King asked to be given Wisdom as the greatest gift that God could give him, and in the ancient Hebrew of the Book of Solomon we can yet read his inspiring words:

I thank Thee, O Great Creator of the Universe, that Thou has taught me the secrets of the Planets that I mayst know the Time and Seasons of Things, the secrets of men's hearts, their thoughts, and the nature of their being. Thou gavest unto me this knowledge which is the foundation of all my Wisdom.

It is these self-same 'Secrets of the Planets' that I have endeavoured to teach in these pages.

I now ask my readers to give their attention and concentration to the following system which I will put as briefly and in as clear language as possible.

To find the exact day in any month of the year whose vibration will be favourable, or in other words 'lucky' to any individual, the simplest rule is to work out by the following table the occult number produced by the letters of their name.

This ancient Chaldean and Hebrew alphabet sets out the number of value of each letter. It is the best system I know for this purpose; its origin is lost in antiquity, but it is believed that it was originated by the Chaldeans, who were masters in all magical arts, and by them passed to the Hebrews.

It will be seen that there is no number 9 given in the alphabet following, for the simple reason that those ancient masters of Occultism knew that in the 'Highest Sphere' the number 9 represents the 9-lettered name of God, and for this reason no single letter was ascribed to it.

If, however, the letters in a name should total up and produce the number 9, the meaning of it is that given as I set out in the previous chapter dealing with the number 9, and for the compound numbers of the 9 such as the 18, 27, etc.

A	=	1	G	=	3	N	=	5	T	=	4
B	=	2	H	=	5	O	=	7	U	=	6
C	=	3	I or J	=	1	P	=	8	V	=	6
D	=	4	K	=	2	Q	=	1	W	=	6
E	=	5	L	=	3	R	=	2	X	=	5
F	=	8	M	=	4	S	=	3	Y	=	1
									Z		7

The next important question to answer is the following: Are all the Christian and Surnames to be added together to find the last digit or number?

The answer to that is, that it is *the most used* Christian and Surname that must be added together to give the Key number; when the Surname is more used or more in evidence than the Christian name, then it is taken to give the key number.

I have only space in a book of this description to give illustrations of a few well-known names. One I will take was always spoken of as Lloyd George—the other, Ex-Prime Minister, was called simply Baldwin.

Lloyd George

The names Lloyd George and the Ex-Prime Minister of England, if transcribed into numbers are as follows:

						B	=	2
			G	=	3	A	=	1
L	=	3	E	=	5	L	=	3
L	=	3	O	=	7	D	=	4
O	=	7	R	=	2	W	=	6
Y	=	1	G	=	3	I	=	1
D	=	4	E	=	5	N	=	5
		18=9			25=7			22=4

In Lloyd George's case, the word Lloyd alone produces the single number of 9, which, as I have previously explained, is connected with persons who have a hard fight with circumstances in their early lives and who, if they rise to positions of authority in nations, are often the cause of wars or (as with Lloyd George) play an active part in them.

The word George in itself produces the single number of 7. This is, as I have also previously explained, a magnetic number, and favourable if used by itself. In this case, however, the two names are never used alone, but always together, as Lloyd George: now add the two single numbers of each name together—7 plus 9 and you get *the compound number of* 16, the occult symbolism of which is 'a Shattered Citadel' or 'a Lightning-struck Tower.' A full description of the compound numbers will be found later in these pages.

If, however, the word David were added it would produce another 7, and if the name David Lloyd George was employed *in continuous use* instead of Lloyd George, the addition of the 7 for the word David would make the total of the three names the number 23, which, as will be seen in Chapter 4 dealing with the meaning of the compound numbers, is considered a fortunate number.

However, by some hidden law of destiny over which man has no control, he became known and called Lloyd George, and so his name foreshadowed that he would one day in his marvellous career fulfil the symbolism of 'a Shattered Citadel' or 'a Lightning-struck Tower.'

The other Ex-Prime Minister was for some unknown reason never called by his political followers or the general public anything else but Baldwin. This name, as you will notice, totals up to the number 22, and in its single figure to a 4.

The number 4, as I explained in a previous chapter, is not considered a fortunate number; people under it are usually misunderstood. They work hard and strive earnestly to carry out their ideas, but their plans are difficult and usually meet with great opposition.

Taking again these two well-known public leaders for another illustration, I now come to the most curious side of this study of numerology, namely, that the 'compound' numbers have an *extraordinary meaning of their own*, which throws an added light on the mysterious connection they have in the still deeper side of occultism as applied to people's names.

Taking again the name Lloyd George, we find the first word Lloyd gives the 'compound' number 18. In occult symbolism this number is represented as 'a rayed moon from which blood is dropping like rain; in a field below a wolf and a dog are catching drops of blood in their opened months.'

Taking the word George, the 'compound' number is 25. In symbolism this number is classed as 'a number of strength gained by experience and ultimate gain through strife.'

The conclusion therefore is that if Lloyd George had become known in the world as plain George he would have retained to the end the high position he had gained.

Lloyd George was born on January 17th; he was therefore by his birth a number 8 man, which is unfortunately not in harmonious vibration with his name number, and further, by being an 8, increases the fatalistic indications given by the number of his name—a 16.

The 'compound' number of 22, made by the name Baldwin, in the same occult symbolism of numbers is not at all favourable from a purely worldly sense as a leader of men. The single number of a name, it must be remembered, represents the man or woman *as they appear to be*. The 'double' or 'compound' number represents *the hidden forces that use the man or woman as their instrument*. The symbolism of the number 22 is 'a good man blinded by the folly of others, with a knapsack on his back full of Errors; he offers no defence against a ferocious tiger who is biting him.'

I have, of course, no political leanings in any direction; I merely am your mentor in these studies:

> Sketch your world exactly as it goes—without offence—to friend or foes.

and I have only quoted the symbolism given to these numbers since the most ancient times.

Sir Austen Chamberlain

As Sir Austen Chamberlain was generally spoken of as Austen Chamberlain, his numbers are as follows:

A	=	1	C	=	3
U	=	6	H	=	5
S	=	3	A	=	1
T	=	4	M	=	4

```
E = 5      B = 2
N = 5      E = 5
   —       R = 2
  24 = 6   L = 3
           A = 1
           I = 1
           N = 5
              —
            32 = 5
```

Both the single numbers and the compound numbers in this name are singularly fortunate, especially if used separately, as I have explained in a previous chapter; the number 6 is usually found associated with persons who rise to high positions of authority—especially in political life.

The compound number 24 is also favourable, and in occult symbolism it is put down as a number that brings 'the assistance and association of people of high rank, and gain through such association.'

The simple number of 5, as in the name Chamberlain, is, as I said on a previous page, a 'lucky' number, especially for those who lead changeable lives with a large element of risk, change, and speculation involved in their career; while the compound number of 32 is also given in occult symbolism as a magical number and is put down as associated with what is called 'the Paths of Wisdom.'

His title of 'Sir' produces the number 6, again a favourable number, and we now add the single numbers of all the three together, we get 6 plus 6 plus 5 equals 17, a compound number whose occult symbolism is curiously enough the 8-pointed Star of Venus, a symbol of Peace and Love, which is peculiarly suitable for the career of a man who made superhuman efforts towards bringing peace between nations at Locarno. If, however, he was only known as Austen Chamberlain, the total of these two words produce the number 11, which, as my readers will see farther on, gives warning of 'hidden dangers, trial and treachery from others.'

Sir Austen Chamberlain was born on October 16th. Neither the single number of 7 nor the compound are in harmonious vibration with the number of his name. This was not a favourable promise for a successful ending of his career, as is explained later on in these pages.

Ramsay MacDonald

We will take the first Labour Prime Minister of England for our next illustration. His numbers are as follows:

R	=	2	M	=	4
A	=	1	A	=	1
M	=	4	C	=	3
S	=	3	D	=	4
A	=	1	O	=	7
Y	=	1	N	=	5
		12=3	A	=	1
			L	=	3
			D	=	4
					32=5

It will be seen that the name Ramsay produces 3 as its simple number and 12 for its compound number.

As I have explained earlier in this book, the single number denotes the person *as he appears to be* in the eyes of his fellow mortals, while the compound number represents the hidden forces in the background of the career.

In this case, the single number '3 is strong and powerful, and is generally associated with ambitious people who gain positions of authority and who do especially well in government departments.

The occult symbolism of the compound number 12, is, however, that of 'the Victim or the Sacrifice.'

The letters of the name MacDonald produce the single number of 5, an excellent number, as I explained before, and the compound number 32 is, as in the case of Sir Austen Chamberlain, also a good number with its symbolism of 'the Paths of Wisdom.'

The addition, however, of the two single numbers of the name Ramsay MacDonald, 5 plus 3, produces an 8, a number which, I have explained earlier, represents two worlds, the material and the spiritual, one side associated with philosophic thought, concentration of purpose and zeal for any cause espoused, the other representing upheavals and revolutions.

This combination, taken with the meaning of the compound number that stands for his Christian name giving the symbolism of 'the Victim or the Sacrifice,' foreshadowed very clearly that Ramsay MacDonald, no matter what his great qualities, would in the end be made 'the victim' or 'the sacrifice' of his political party and be associated in his career with upheavals and revolutions.

The addition of the numbers of the two names 12 and 32 produces the compound numbers of 44, which in the explanation of compound numbers given in Chapter 4 reads: 'This number is full of the gravest warnings for the future. It foreshadows disasters brought about by association with others'. A decidedly ominous indication of the future of the leader of one of England's political parties. Further, as he was born on October 12th, the single number of which is a 3, this is not in harmonious vibration with his Name number, an 8. Consequently one might have expected a great deal of muddle and jumble to be associated with his career.

If this man had really understood the extraordinary meaning there is in a name when transcribed into numbers, he would never have allowed his party or his public to call him by the single word Ramsay. He should never have allowed such familiarity, but insisted on being called, *if he could do it*, by the single word MacDonald with its magical number of 32.

Later on in this book (Chapter 22) will be found examples from the names of Presidents of the United States.

In the following chapter I will explain the symbolism that from the most ancient times has been given to what is called 'compound numbers,' and at the same time I will give the system I have alluded to at the beginning of this chapter, whereby readers will be able to understand how it is that they can know when the 'lucky' day comes, so that they may be able to take hold of any good opportunity which may present itself.

4

The 'Compound' or 'Spiritual' Numbers Fully Described

IN THE PRECEDING CHAPTERS I have given the meanings of what are called the principal or 'single' numbers—also called the 'root' numbers—from 1 to 9. I will now proceed with the next step in this curious study of Numerology, namely, the explanation of the occult symbolism given to what are called the 'double' or 'compound' numbers, and how such knowledge may be made use of in everyday life.

Although this is a much more advanced and more difficult part of the study of numbers, I will endeavour to make it as clear and as easy to understand as I have endeavoured to do with the single numbers in the earlier chapters.

Before launching out into this side of the subject, I must, I feel, give a few words of explanation so as to prepare my readers for what is to follow.

I have already explained that the single numbers denote what the man or woman *appears to be* in the eyes of their fellow mortals, while the double or compound numbers show the hidden influences that play their role behind the scenes as it were, and in some mysterious way often foreshadow the future or the hidden current of destiny of the individual.

When one passes the major or root numbers of 1 to 9, what is called the greater symbolism of numbers commences, and continues until 5 times 9 is reached, or the number 45; at this point the mystical number of 7 is brought into operation and added to the number of 45, producing 52, which stands for the 52 weeks of a year. This number of 52, multiplied by 7, gives 364 as the ordinary days of the year in that ancient period of Time when trade unionism had not made its appearance. These ancient and wonderful people, however used the 365th day of each year as *the one great festival holiday of all*, and *no work of any kind* was allowed to be done by man, woman, child, or beast. This number of 365 is based on the passage of the Sun through the twelve divisions of the Zodiac, which is the origin of the calculation of the year period which is found in every civilisation.

As I said before, the meaning of the single numbers from 1 to 9 represents how the man or woman appears in the eyes of his fellows. They are the numbers of *individuality and personality*.

All numbers from 10 up become in symbolism 'double' or 'compound' numbers; the 12, if we take it for an example, has for its root or fadic number a single number such as the 3, but at the same time the 1 and 2 of which the twelve is composed are 'compound' and have a meaning of their own distinct from the number 3.

How and in what age these 'compound' numbers became illustrated by symbolism, we do not know and never can know. We can only say that they appear to have always existed.

Symbols may be called the Language of Nature, and as such we must take them.

The meanings ascribed to the numbers 1 to 9 belong then to *the physical or material side of things*, and 'compound' numbers from 10 on belong to the more *occult or spiritual side of life*. Distinct symbolism has been given to the 'compound' numbers up to that mysterious number of 52, and this symbolism I will now proceed to give in as clear language as it may be possible to translate them. I have already illustrated in a previous chapter by examples from names such as Lloyd George, Baldwin, Austen Chamberlain, and Ramsay MacDonald, the information one is able to get by knowing the meaning of the 'compound' number and using it in relation to the information given by the single number, but later on it will be my privilege to explain a still more practical application of this knowledge which will enable one actually to pick out what days will be fortunate and what will be unfortunate, which will be, I think, of inestimable value to my readers.

The universally accepted symbolism of the compound numbers in ancient times was given in pictures and may still be found in the Tarot cards which have been handed down to us from the most distant ages and whose origin is lost in antiquity.

10: Symbolised as the 'Wheel of Fortune.' It is a number of honour, of faith and self-confidence, of rise and fall; one's name will be known for good or evil, according to one's desires; it is a fortunate number in the sense that one's plans are likely to be carried out.

11: This is an ominous number to occultists. It gives warning of hidden dangers, trial, and treachery from others. It has a symbol of 'a Clenched Hand,' and 'a Lion Muzzled,' and of a person who will have great difficulties to contend against.

12: The symbolism of this number is suffering and anxiety of mind. It is also indicated as 'the sacrifice of the Victim' and generally foreshadows one being sacrificed for the plans or intrigues of others.

13: This is a number indicating change of plans, place, and such-like, and is not unfortunate, as is generally supposed. In some of the ancient writings it is said, 'He who understands the number 13 will be given power and dominion.' It is symbolised by the picture of 'a Skeleton' or 'Death,' with a scythe reaping down men, in a field of new-grown grass where young faces and heads appear cropping up on every side. It is a number of upheaval and destruction. It is a symbol of 'Power' which if wrongly used will wreak destruction upon itself. It is a number of warning of the unknown or unexpected, if it becomes a 'compound' number in one's calculations.

14: This is a number of movement, combination of people and things, and danger from natural forces, such as tempests, water, air, or fire. This number is fortunate for dealings with money, speculation, and changes in business, but there is always a strong element of risk and danger attached to it, but generally owing to the actions and foolhardiness of others. If this number comes out in calculations of future events the person should be warned to act with caution and prudence.

15: This is a number of occult significance, of magic and mystery; but as a rule it does not represent the higher side of occultism, its meaning being that the persons represented by it will use every art of magic they can to carry out their purpose. If associated with a good or fortunate single number, it can be very lucky and powerful, but if associated with one of the peculiar numbers, such as a 4 or an 8, the person it represents will not scruple to use any sort of art, or even 'black magic,' to gain what he or she desires.

It is peculiarly associated with 'good takers,' often

eloquence, gifts of Music and Art and a dramatic personality, combined with a certain voluptuous temperament and strong personal magnetism. For obtaining money, gifts, and favours from others it is a fortunate number.

16: This number has a most peculiar occult symbolism. It is pictured by 'a Tower Struck by Lightning from which a man is falling with a Crown on his head.' It is also called 'the Shattered Citadel.'

It gives warning of some strange fatality awaiting one, also danger of accidents and defeat of one's plans. If it appears as a 'compound' number relating to the future, it is a warning sign that should be carefully noted and plans made in advance in the endeavour to avert its fatalistic tendency.

17: This is a highly spiritual number, and is expressed in symbolism by the 8-pointed star of Venus; a symbol of 'Peace and Love.' It is also called 'the Star of the Magi' and expresses that the person it represents has risen superior in spirit to the trials and difficulties of his life or his career. It is considered a 'number of immortality' and that the person's name 'lives after him.' It is a fortunate number if it works out in relation to future events, provided it is not associated with the single numbers of fours and eights.

18: This number has a difficult symbolism to translate. It is pictured as 'a rayed moon from which drops of blood are falling; a wolf and a hungry dog are seen below catching the falling drops of blood in their opened mouths, while still lower a crab is seen hastening to join them.' It is symbolic of materialism striving to destroy the spiritual side of the nature. It generally associates a person with bitter quarrels, even family ones, also with war, social upheavals, revolutions; and in some cases it indicates making money and position through wars or by wars. It is, however, a warning of treachery, deception by others, also danger from the elements, such as storms, danger from water, fires, and explosions. When this 'compound' number appears in working out dates in advance, such a date should be taken with a great amount of care, caution, and circumspection.

19: This number is regarded as fortunate and extremely favourable. It is symbolised as 'the Sun' and is called 'the Prince of Heaven.' It is a number promising happiness, success, esteem, and honour, and promises success in one's plans for the future.

20: This number is called 'the Awakening'; also 'the Judgement.' It is symbolised by the figure of a winged angel sounding a trumpet, while from below a man, a woman and a child are seen rising from a tomb with their hands clasped in prayer.

This number has a peculiar interpretation: the awakening of new purpose, new plans, new ambitions, the call to action, but for some great purpose, cause, or duty. It is not a material number and consequently is a doubtful one as far as wordly success is concerned.

If used in relation to a future event, it denotes delays, hindrances to one's plans, which can only be conquered through the development of the spiritual side of the nature.

21: This number is symbolised by the picture of 'the Universe,' and it is also called 'the Crown of the Magi.' It is a number of advancement, honours, elevation in life, and general success. It means victory after a long fight, for 'the Crown of the Magi' is only gained after long initiation and tests of determination. It is a fortunate number of promise if it appears in any connection with future events.

22: This number is symbolised by 'a Good Man

blinded by the folly of others, with a knapsack on his back full of Errors'. In this picture he appears to offer no defence against a ferocious tiger which is attacking him. It is a warning number of illusion and delusion, a good person who lives in a fool's paradise; a dreamer of dreams who awakens only when surrounded by danger. It is also a number of false judgment owing to the influence of others.

As a number in connection with future events its warning and meaning should be carefully noted.

23: This number is called 'the Royal Star of the Lion.' It is a promise of success, help from superiors and protection from those in high places. In dealing with future events it is a most fortunate number and a promise of success for one's plans.

24: This number is also fortunate; it promises the assistance and association of those of rank and position with one's plans; it also denotes gain through love and the opposite sex; it is a favourable number when it comes out in relation to future events.

25: This is a number denoting strength gained through experience, and benefits obtained through observation of people and things. It is not deemed exactly 'lucky,' as its success is given through strife and trials in the earlier life. It is favourable when it appears in regard to the future.

26: This number is full of the gravest warnings for the future. It foreshadows disasters brought about by association with others; run, by bad speculations, by partnerships, unions, and bad advice.

If it comes out in connection with future events one should carefully consider the path one is treading.

27: This is a good number and is symbolised as 'the Sceptre.' It is a promise of authority, power, and command. It indicates that reward will come from the productive intellect; that the creative faculties have sown goods seeds that will reap a harvest. Persons with this 'compound' number at their back should carry out their own ideas and plans. It is a fortunate number if it appears in any connection with future events.

28: This number is full of contradictions. It indicates a person of great promise and possibilities who is likely to see all taken away from him unless he carefully provides for the future. It indicates loss through trust in others, opposition and competition in trade, danger of loss through law, and the likelihood of having to begin life's road over and over again.

It is not a fortunate number for the indication of future events.

29: This number indicates uncertainties, treachery, and deception of others; it foreshadows trials, tribulation, and unexpected dangers, unreliable friends, and grief and deception caused by members of the opposite sex. It gives grave warning if it comes out in anything concerning future events.

30: This is a number of thoughtful deduction, retrospection, and mental superiority over one's fellows, but, as it seems to belong completely to the mental plane, the persons it represents are likely to put all material things on one side—not because they have to, but because they wish to do so. For this reason it is neither fortunate nor unfortunate, for either depends on the mental outlook of the person it represents. It can be all powerful, but it is just as often indifferent according to the will or desire of the person.

31: This number is very similar to the preceding one, except that the person it represents is even more self-contained, lonely, and isolated from his fellows. It is not a fortunate number from a worldly or material standpoint.

32. This number has a magical power like the single 5, or the 'compound' numbers 14 and 23. It is usually associated with combinations of people or nations. It is a fortunate number if the person it represents holds to his own judgment and opinions; if not, his plans are likely to become wrecked by the stubbornness and stupidity of others. It is a favourable number if it appears in connection with future events.

33: This number has no potency of its own, and consequently has the same meaning as the 24—which is also a 6—and the next to it in its own series of 'compound' numbers.

34: Has the same meaning as the number 25, which is the next to it in its own series of 'compound' numbers.

35: Has the same meaning as the number 26, which is the next to it in its own series of 'compound' numbers.

36: Has the same meaning as the number 27, which is the next to it in its own series of 'compound' numbers.

37: This number has a distinct potency of its own. It is a number of good and fortunate friendships in love and in combination connected with the opposite sex. It is also good for partnerships of all kinds. It is a fortunate indication if it appears in connection with future events.

38: Has the same meaning as the number 29, which is the next to it in its own series of 'compound' numbers.

39: Has the same meaning as the number 30, which is the next to it in its own series of 'compound' numbers.

40: Has the same meaning as the number 31,

which is next to it in its own series of 'compound' numbers.

41: Has the same meaning as the number 32, which is next to it in its own series of 'compound' numbers.

42: Has the same meaning as the number 24.

43: This is an unfortunate number. It is symbolised by the sign of revolution, upheaval, failure, and prevention, and is not a fortunate number if it comes out in calculations relating to future events.

44: Has the same meaning as 26.

45: Has the same meaning as 27.

46: Has the same meaning as 37.

47: Has the same meaning as 29.

48: Has the same meaning as 30.

49: Has the same meaning as 31.

50: Has the same meaning as 32.

51: This number has a very powerful potency of its own. It represents the nature of the warrior; it promises sudden advancement in whatever one undertakes; it is especially favourable for those in military or naval life and for leaders in any cause. At the same time it threatens enemies, danger, and the likelihood of assassination.

52: Has the same meaning as 43.

We have now completed the 52 numbers which represent the 52 weeks of our year, and for all practical purposes there is no necessity to proceed farther. I will now show my readers the method of employing the symbolism of these 'compound' numbers, together with the 'single' numbers whose meaning they have learned earlier in this book.

The rule to follow is: One must add the date one wishes to know about to the total of the compound numbers of one's name, see what number this gives one and read the meaning I have given to the added number.

Example

I will suppose you wish to know if, say, Monday the 26th April will be a favourable day for you to carry out some plan: let us say, to ask for a rise in your position or in your wages. Take the number given to each letter of your name from the alphabet I have shown you, add to the total 'compound' number or its single digit the number given by the addition of the 26th April, 2 plus 6 and 8, add this 8 to the total of your Name number and Birth number and look up the meaning I have given to the final number produced, and you will find at once whether Monday, the 26th, will be favourable to you or not. If you see that it does not give a fortunate number, then add the next day, the 27th, or the next until you come to a date *that is indicated as favourable*. Act on the favourable date thus shown, and you will find that the day thus indicated will be be fortunate for you.

Suppose your name to be John Smith born 8th January, work the name out as follows:

J	=	1	S	=	3
O	=	7	M	=	4
H	=	5	I	=	1
N	=	5	T	=	4
		—	H	=	5
	18	= 9			—
				17	= 8

Example

You now add the 9 and the 8 together, which gives you the 'compound' number of 17, whose units added together give 8. To this add the 8 produced by similar means from the 26th April, this gives you the number 16, with 7 for the single number; now add the Birth number 8th January to this 7 and you obtain 15 for the last compound number with 6 for the last single number.

Look up the meaning I have given to the compound Number 15: you will find it stated 'for obtaining money, gifts, and favours from others, it is fortunate number.' Therefore the occult influences playing on John Smith, born 8th January, would be favourable on the 26th April for his using that date to ask favours or carrying out his plans. If it had not given favourable indications 'John Smith' should then work out the 27th April, or the next day or the next, until he found a date indicated as fortunate.

The same rule applies for every name and every date of birth.

5

More Information on How to Use 'Single' and 'Compound' Numbers

FOLLOWING THE PUBLICATION of some articles I published in a leading London paper, I received some thousands of letters asking for further information as to how to make the Birth number and the Name number accord. I have, therefore, worked out the following example.

If possible, make the Birth number and the number given by the Name agree; the vibrations will then all be in harmony and will give a greater promise of success if the number is a favourable one.

As an illustration, take again the example I gave in the previous chapter, of John Smith:

J	=	1	S	=	3
O	=	7	M	=	4
H	=	5	I	=	1
N	=	5	T	=	4
		—	H	=	5
	18 = 1 plus 8 = 9				—
				17 = 1 plus 7 = 8

The single number of John totals a 9, and the single number of Smith equals an 8; the 8 and 9 added together make 17, and 1 plus 7 makes 8. The number of the entire Name is therefore an 8. If John Smith were born on any day making an 8, such as the 8th, 17th, or 26th of a month, the number of the Name and the number of the Birth *would then be in harmony*, and although the 8 is not such a lucky number to have in an ordinary way, yet in such a case there would be *no clash in the numbers*; and if John Smith, knowing this, used the dates making an 8, such as the 8th, 17th, or 26th, for his important transactions, he would find himself more fortunate.

If, on the contrary, he had another number, say 2, as his Birth number, such as the 2nd, 11th, 20th, or 29th, his Name and his Birth number would *not be in vibration one to the other* and there would always be a muddle or jumble in his affairs, and he would also not be able to decide which number to act on or what date he should use.

As he cannot alter his Birth number, then the thing to do is to alter the *Name number*. If he added a letter making a 3 to his name, such as a C, a G, an L, or an S, which in the Alphabet I gave in a previous chapter have the number 3, and wrote his name, say, 'John C. Smith,' or 'John G. Smith,' and, insisted on being known and called as that, this new Number 3, added to the 17, which John Smith made before, would now give a total of 20, or a single number of 2, and then both the Name number and the Birth number *would be in harmonious vibration together*, and he would also be sure that he would be right in selecting any date that makes a 2, such as the 2nd, 11th, 20th, or 29th, of any month, as the most favourable day to make any change or carry out any important plan.

If, however, 'John Smith' was born under an 8, such as the 8th, 17th, or 26th of any month, as the total of the numbers of his name also make an 8, I would then not advise him to add a letter or change the Name number, but to work under the 8, as I explained earlier.

However, if a person is born under either of those peculiar numbers such as a 4 or an 8, and if the Name number should also total up to a 4 when one is born under an 8, or to an 8 when one is born under a 4, then for material success it would be better if one added some letter, as I explained in the case of John Smith, so that the total of your number is no longer a 4 or an 8, but one with a more fortunate vibration, making, say, a 1, 3, 6, or 9. Such a change in the majority of cases will produce most fortunate results and set up entirely new vibrations, which will change a lonely, unlucky life into one of happiness and success.

I would also strongly advise all those who have the combination of 4 and 8 when they make the change by altering their name to produce another number, such as a 1, 3, 6, or 9, to wear the colours and jewels I have set out for these numbers in an earlier chapter in this book dealing with 'single' numbers, and I am absolutely confident that they will never regret having followed my advice.

I also advise that in order to get the best advantage out of one's numbers, that in living in cities and towns a person should select a house to live in whose number also gives the same vibration as the Birth and Name number. If they live in the country they should give a name to their house which produces the same number as the Birth and Name. Especially in the case of a person having an 8 for the Birth number and a 4 for the Name number, or vice versa, they should, under no circumstances, live in a house whose number worked out to the single digit of a 4 or an 8.

6

Why the Birth Number is Most Important

THE BIRTH NUMBER is the easiest and clearest to use for everyday matters, and for all those who are not advanced students in occult symbolism. It indicates with authority and decision the exact date for action, namely a date which will be *in accord and harmony with the Birth number*, and the rules concerning it are simple and easy to understand.

A person born on, say, the 1st, 10th, 19th, or 28th, of any month will be quite safe in picking out any one of these dates as the best date for any important action. As the number 4 is what may be called the feminine or negative side of the 1, he or she can take this number as *an associate number*, but on account of the peculiar qualities of this number 1 I do not advise it to be chosen for any *worldly or material affairs*. This number 4 will generally be found by number 1 persons as coming into their lives 'on its own,' if I may be permitted to describe its action as such, but more in the nature of a fatalistic number which has an influence on their lives *outside of their control* and certainly not always connected with the happier side of life. In many instances of number 1 people in my collection, the number 4, such as the 4th, 13th, 22nd, and 31st, has brought on these dates the news of an accident, a death, or a sorrow which has played some important part in their lives. The number 1 people also often find that they seem unconsciously to be drawn to live in houses whose number makes a 4, such as a house in a terrace or street numbered 4, 13, 22, 31, 40, 49, etc., and although such houses may be proved to be associated with important events in the career, yet I have seldom found them associated with happy *material* advantages.

A person whose Birth number is an 8 should certainly never live in a house whose number makes a 4, 13, 22, 31, 40, etc., and neither should a person whose Birth number makes a 4 live in a house whose number makes an 8, 17, 26, 35, 44, etc., not, at least, if they wish to escape sorrow, misfortune, and strange fatality.

The second best numbers for a person whose Birth number makes a 1 are the interchangeable numbers of the 2—7, and dates these numbers make, such as the 2nd 7th, 11th, 16th, 20th, 25th, or 29th, and houses under the numbers 2, 7, 11, 16, 20, 25, 29, 34, etc., are generally not unfavourable; but as these numbers are related to change or unsettled conditions, the number 1 person seldom settles down in houses under the 2—7 numbers, or finds conditions brought into his or her life under the dates given by these numbers as relating to *fixed or settled matters*.

Under the law of harmony and vibration, there is no question but that number 1 persons should be associated as much as possible with the same number 2 in all its forms. Persons born under the 3 should employ their number 3, and so on for all the numbers with the exception of those born under the 4 and the 8. In the latter cases I recommend, then, *not to increase* the peculiar influence of the 4 and 8, but to choose more fortunate vibrations.

This is where the power and knowledge of the

Name number will apply. A number 4 or a number 8 person who desires to get under more fortunate vibrations, as they cannot alter their Birth number they can at least *change their Name number* and live under it and so become equally as fortunate as those whose Birth number is a lucky one.

I will give an example of what I mean.

Suppose a man or woman has been born on, say, the 8th, 17th, or 26th of January, and the Name number works out, let us say, to a final total of a 1, 3, 5, or 6 (I have purposely taken the strong or positive numbers.) Then I most certainly advise the number 8 persons to drop using the 8 in all their transactions and use instead any strong number *the name may give*, such as a 1, 3, 5, or 6, and a number 4 person should do likewise.

You will notice I have not used the 9 in giving this rule, and my reason for not doing so is that the 4, which is the symbol of the Planet Uranus, and the 8, which represents the Planet Saturn, are so antagonistic in their qualities to the 9, the symbol of Mars, that it is better to keep such numbers apart.

This may sound strange to those who have not made any study of occultism, but believe me, the above rule is not laid down at random or by any shadowy guess-work; on the contrary, it has a solid foundation in the science of the Planets, and anyone who has ever studied Astrology will tell you that I am right when I say that any combination of the Planets of Mars (9) and Saturn (8) or Uranus (4) can only foreshadow troubles and disasters of all kinds.

7

Some Illustrations of Names and Numbers

As it is impossible in a book of this size to go into every shade of the occult significance of numbers that spring from the foundation of 1 to 9, I must confine myself to giving a few illustrations of how to use the numbers allotted to the letters of the Hebrew alphabet for the purpose of showing how Destiny appears interwoven with numbers and names.

The great Napoleon originally wrote his name as Napoleon Buonaparte. Later on in his life he changed it to Napoleon Bonaparte. This change had a curious significance:

        Napoleon equals in numbers 5
        Buonaparte equals in numbers 5

The number 5, as I showed earlier in these pages, is considered a magical number and was carried by the ancient Greeks as a mascot when they went into battle. The two numbers of 5, if added, producing 10, are equally important and strangely significant in this case.

When Napoleon altered the spelling to Bonaparte, it altered the vibration of this word to an 8, and if you refer to what I said about this number you will find on the lower plane it represents revolution, anarchy, waywardness, conflict with human justice, and on the lower plane a tragic ending to the life. Although a great man, Napoleon was on the lower plane of existence, as can be seen if one looks up how the number 8 (Saturn) and the 9 (Mars) dominated the chief events of his career. As Napoleon Bonaparte the two names total the number 13, which number, in the occult symbolism which accompanies this system of letters and numbers, bears the curious picture of a skeleton with a scythe *mowing men down*, also a symbol of 'Power' which 'if wrongly used will bring destruction upon itself.' This was so borne out by Napoleon's career that further comment is unnecessary. Some remarkable illustrations of the significance of names and numbers may be had from examples of ships.

The United States battleship *Maine*, which so mysteriously exploded in Havana Harbour, and in which every man on board was lost, gives for the word 'Maine' the number 16 for its compound number, the symbolism for this number being, as you will have read earlier, 'A Tower Struck by Lightning.' The mystery of the blowing up of this warship has never been solved, but it caused the declaration of war by the United States against Spain.

Another tragic ship disaster was that of the *Waratah* which, after leaving Australia, sank with all her passengers and crew as if she had been swallowed up by the ocean. The number of the word 'Waratah' equals 20, which, as you have read in Chapter 4, is called 'the Judgment.' This number is symbolised by the figure of a winged angel sounding a trumpet, while from below a man, a woman, and a child are seen rising from a tomb with their hands clasped in prayer.

8

Examples of How Numbers Recur in Lives

AMONG MY COLLECTION on the influence of numbers in connection with events, I have many that are decidedly interesting.

The following appeared in many of the London newspapers: Sir Alma-Tadema, the famous artist, says his important number is 17. He was 17 when he first met his wife; their first house had that number; it was on August 17th that the work of rebuilding his home began, and on November 17th that he took up his residence there. His second marriage was in 1871,—and here 17 is the result of the figures added together. His house, in the artistic quarter of St. John's Wood, was again a multiple of 17. Sir Alma-Tadema was born on January 8th, which would account for the 17th, which gives the single number 8, having such importance in his life.

King Edward VII was born on the 9th November in a month that is called in Astrology 'the second house of Mars' and governed by 9, the number of Mars.

His marriage took place in the year 1863, which numbers added to the other make 9; he was to have been crowned on the 27th of June, which figures together make 9, and he was actually crowned on August 9th.

King Edward often referred to me 'as the man who would not let him live past 69.' On the occasion when

I first had the honour of meeting him as Prince of Wales in Lady Arthur Paget's house, he asked me to 'work out his numbers.' I did so and explained the reason his 'fadic' or 'root' numbers were the 6 and the 9. I then told him that when these two numbers came together would be his fatal year, and further than the event should take place on a day making the number 6 in a month governed by the 6, which would be May. He never forgot my prediction, and it is my melancholy privilege to record that the last occasion when I had any conversation with his late Majesty was a few weeks before his death. He was joining the royal train at Victoria to make his usual journey to the Continent when he noticed me I happened also to be going abroad. He sent an equerry to call me, and he said, smiling broadly:

'Well, "Cheiro," I'm still alive, as you see, but from that warning of yours, as I am now in my 69th year, I must take care'—a reference to the fact that according to the fadic system of numbers his 69th year was for him a dangerous year. He then spoke briefly of his racing wagers, and concluded by emphasing how remarkably my advice had been crowned by success.

Alas, in a few short weeks he returned to Buckingham Palace, and the public heard with consternation of his illness, which proved fatal. On May 6th—in his 69th year, the first time that these 'fadic' numbers came together—my prediction was fulfilled.

Incidentally, King Edward mentioned that his 'dear friend,' as he called him, Lord Randolph Churchill, was extremely superstitious in regard to the number 13, and attributed many adverse events to the fact that he was born on the 13th of February, 1849, the total of whose numbers 22 also made a 4.

I explained to King Edward that the idea that 13 was an unfortunate number was not supported by occultism; that it was in fact an important number if persons were born on the 4th 13th, 22nd, or 31st, and it was simply regarded as ill-omened because in occultism it was looked upon with veneration.

A few years before his death in London in January, 1895, I had a brief interview with this famous statesman and he reminded me that my theory of numbers had interested him very much. From King Edward he had gathered that I thought that 4 was his fadic number and I confirmed this. It was also represented with almost all the leading events of his life.

Another remarkable instance of prediction by numbers was in the case of my meeting with the then Sir Charles Russell. I explained to him that his important numbers were the 1 and the 4, with what are called their interchangeable numbers of 2 and 7, and that he would reach the highest position his career could give him on a date that made a 1, such as the 1st, 10th, 19th, or 28th in a month governed by the 2 and 7, such as July, which is governed by those numbers, and in a year whose numbers added up to the number of 4. He made a careful note of this, and when he wore his robes of Lord Chief Justice of England for the first time he sent for me to come to the Law Courts. After the ceremony of installation was over he came to me in his private room and as a souvenir gave me a signed impression of his hand.

9

The Dread of the '13' Unfounded

NEARLY ALL PEOPLE have an extraordinary dread of the number 13, which, if they only knew the real truth, is not at all the unlucky number they imagine it to be.

The origin of this dread is due primarily to the fact that it was much used in connection with occultism, and was in far-off times regarded as a powerful although a fatalistic number. As I stated before in previous pages, in some of the old writings of famous Adepts it is said, 'He who understands the number 13 hath the Keys of power and dominion.'

The opposition of the early Church to occultism was one of the principal reasons why this number became 'taboo.' It was given out that as 13 sat down to the Last Supper it would be unlucky if 13 were to eat together, and that one of the 13 would die within the year, and so forth.

I must say I could never see the logic of this, for if Christ had not been crucified the Scriptures would not 'have been fulfilled,' in which case Christianity would never have existed.

There was another reason, however, why 13 was dreaded, and this was because the occult symbolism that stood for this number was represented by a mystic picture of 'a skeleton with a scythe in its bony hands reaping down men.'

It was a curious picture that few could understand,

and those who did kept their knowledge to themselves in an age when even to speak of such things was to forfeit one's life by torture or at the stake.

This picture allotted to the number 13, although drawn or painted in many different ways, always contained the same idea: a skeleton reaping in a field, hands and feet springing up among new-grown grass, the crowned head of a man fallen at the point of the scythe, while a female head with flowing hair parted in the centre appeared in the background.

To find the true interpretation of this weird picture one must go back to the meaning attached to the single number 4, of which the 13 makes a second 4 in its compound number.

The single 4, as you have read earlier in these pages, is a strange number in itself. Persons dominated by it are usually misunderstood and lonely in their lives; people who bring about opposition with secret enemies constantly at work against them; they reverse the order of things in communities and governments; they are attracted to social questions and reforms of all kinds; they rebel against authority and set up new dynasties or republics.

The 13 has all these qualities in its higher scale, but even more accentuated. It cuts down all before it, reversing the order of things shown by the hands and feet springing up in the grass and the crowned head falling before the scythe. The female head in the background denotes social reform, the new order of things, and the uplifting of woman, and so forth.

It was perhaps this picture of a skeleton with a scythe in its bony fingers, calling up the idea of Death in the minds of those who could not understand the inner meaning of the symbolism, that caused the number 13 to be so dreaded.

If people will, however, only think, they will see that the 13 belongs to the series of 4, in the range of 4, 13, 22, 31, etc., and consequently a person born, say, on the 4th, 13,th 22nd, or 31st of a month will find all these numbers recurring in their careers, and this being so, the 13 will crop up just as often as the other numbers which make a 4.

In many hotels, even the modern ones, there is no Room 13th; and a similar peculiarity characterises the seats of opera-houses in Italy.

But the dread of 13 has only a limited geographical range.

In the East and in the West the number is honoured. In the Indian Pantheon there are 13 Buddhas. The mystical discs which surround Indian and Chinese pagodas are 13 in number. Enshrined in the Temple of Atsusa, in Japan, is a sacred sword with 13 objects of mystery forming its hilt. Turning westward, 13 was the sacred number of the Mexicans. They had 13 snake gods.

The original States that formed the American Union were 13; its motto, *E Pluribus Unum*, has 13 letters, the American eagle has 13 feathers in each wing, and when George Washington raised the Republican standard he was saluted with 13 guns.

10

The Extraordinary Example of Numbers in the Lives of St. Louis and Louis XVI

ONE OF THE MOST remarkable instances I have ever come across of numbers pointing to a sequence of similar events in lives as far apart as over five hundred years, and which might be used as evidence of reincarnation, is the extraordinary case of St. Louis of France and King Louis XVI, which was published in 1852 in a book called *Research into the Efficacy of Dates and Names in the Annuals of Nations*.

As history shows, there was an interval of exactly 539 years between the birth of St. Louis and Louis XVI.

If one adds this interval number to the remarkable dates in the life of St. Louis, a parallel of events, even to similarity in names, will be seen in the events in the life of Louis XVI.

St. Louis		Louis XVI	
Birth of St. Louis 23rd April,	1215	Birth of Louis XVI 23rd August,	
Add interval	539		
	1754		1754
Birth of Isabel, sister of St. Louis	1225	Birth of Elizabeth, sister of Louis XVI	
Add interval	539		
	1764		1764

Death of Louis VIII, father of St. Louis. 1226 Add interval 539 ――― 1765	Death of the Dauphin father of Louis XVI 1765
Minority of St. Louis commences 1226 Add interval 539 ――― 1765	Minority of Louis XVI commences 1765
Marriage of St. Louis 1231 Add interval 539 ――― 1770	Marriage of Louis XVI 1770
Majority of St. Louis (King) 1235 Add interval 539 ――― 1774	Accession of Louis XVI, King of France 1774
St. Louis concludes a peace with Henry III 1243 Add interval 539 ――― 1782	Louis XVI concludes a peace with George III 1782
An Eastern prince sends an ambassador to St. Louis desiring to become a Christian 1249 Add interval 539 ――― 1788	An Eastern prince sends an ambassador to Louis XVI for the same purpose 1788
Captivity of St. Louis 1250 Add interval 539 ――― 1789	Louis XVI deprived of all power 1789
St. Louis abandoned 1250 Add interval 539 ――― 1789	Louis XVI abandoned 1789

Bitrh of Tristian (sorrow) 1250 Add interval 539 _____ 1789	Fall of the Bastille and Commencement of the Revolution 1789
Beginning of Pastoral under Jacob 1250 Add interval 539 _____ 1789	Beginning of the Jacobins in France 1789
Death of Isabel d'Angoulême 1250 Add interval 539 _____ 1789	Birth of Isabel d' Angoulême in France 1789
Death of Queen Blanche, mother of St. Louis 1253 Add interval 539 _____ 1792	End of the White Lily of France 1792
St. Louis desires to retire and become a Jacobin 1254 Add interval 539 _____ 1793	Louis XVI quits life at the hands of the Jacobins 1793
St. Louis returns to Madeleine Provence 1254 Add interval 539 _____ 1793	Louis XVI interred in the cemetery of the medeleine in Paris 1793

This, I believe, is one of the most curious examples of history repeating itself at a fixed interval. The addition of the interval number 539 reduced to the single digit gives the number 8, and the number of letters in the name Louis XVI gives also the 8. This number, as I explained earlier, represents the symbol of Justice and of one appealing from the brutality of Human Justice to that of the Divine.

11

Periodicity in Numbers

THE LAW OF PERIODICITY is shown in some lives in a very remarkable manner. In many cases it may last for hundreds of years, as may be noticed in the lives of St. Louis and Louis XVI in the interval of 539 years that separated these two Kings of France, and which interval, when added to the date of important events in St. Louis's life, repeated similar events in the career of Louis XVI. This is considered one of the most curious examples, known in history.

Further, it will be noticed that St. Louis was born on April 23rd, the numbers added together producing a 5. Louis XVI was born August 23rd, also producing a 5.

These names worked out by the Hebrew Alphabet are:

```
    S A I N T                L O U I S
    3 1 1 5 4                3 7 6 1 3
    ─────────                ─────────
      14 = 5                   20 = 2
                            5 and 2 = 7


    L O U I S                  X V I
    3 7 6 1 3                  1 6
    ─────────                  ─────
      20 = 2                     7
                             2 and 7 = 9
```

The name Saint Louis worked out to its single digit gives 7, the spiritual number. Louis XVI worked out to its single digit gives 9, the material number. These two single numbers added together give 16 for the compound number, the occult meaning b ing, as you have read in a previous chapter, 'A Tower Struck by Lightning from which a man is falling with a Crown on his head,' a fitting symbol in every sense for the downfall of Louis XVI.

After this date, the execution of Louis XVI, in 1793, we cannot yet trace this curious law of periodicity farther, but in adding the interval number again to 1793 we get the year 2332, in which perhaps another incarnation of St. Louis will again reign in France.

Another interesting example of a number being associated with the kings of France is the following:

The first King of France named Henri was consecrated on the *14th* May, 1029, and the last king of the name of Henri was assassinated on the *14th* May, 1610.

Fourteen letters it will be found make the name of Henri de Bourbon, who was the *14th* King to bear the title of King of France and Navarre.

On the *14th* December, 1553, or 14 centuries, 14 decades, and 14 years after the birth of Christ, Henri IV of France was born; the figures of the date 1553 added together make also the number 14.

On the *14th* May, 1554, Henri II signed the decree for the enlargement of the Rue de la Ferronnerie. The cause of this order—the narrowness of this street—not having been carried into execution, brought about the assassination of Henri IV *in that same street exactly* 4 *times* 14 *years later*.

On the *14th* May, 1552, Marquerite de Valois, the first wife of Henri IV, was born.

On the *14th* May, 1558, the Duke of Guise opend

the revolt against Henri III.

On the *14th* March, 1590, Henry IV won the important Battle of Ivry.

On the *14th* May, 1590, the main Army of Henry IV was defeated at the Fauxbourg of Paris.

On the *14th* November, 1590, 'the Sixteen' took an oath of death rather than serve Henry IV.

On the *14th* November, 1592, the French Parliament accepted the Papal Bill, which gave authority to the legate of Rome to nominate a king instead of Henry IV.

On the *14th* December, 1599, the Duke of Savoy submitted to Henry IV.

On the *14th* September, the Dauphin, who later became Louis XIII, was baptised.

On the *14th* May, 1643; Louis XIII, the son of Henry IV, died on the same day of the same month that his father was killed, and if the figures of 1643 are added together they make the Number *14*, which had played such an important part in his father's career.

Louis XIV ascended the throne in 1643, also a *14*, and died in 1715, which also makes a *14*. His age at his death was 77, again making by addition a *14*.

Louis XV ascended the throne in 1715=*14*.

Louis XVI was in the *14th* year of his reign when he convoked the States-General, which brought about the Revolution and his downfall.

The reason why this number 14 or its single number 5 appears so much associated with the destiny of France may be traced to the fact that in Astrology Paris has always been represented as governed by the Sign Virgo, whose Planet is Mercury in its negative aspect, whose number is a 5.

During the period of French history I have cited, Paris was the principal point of power. The king who reigned in Paris ruled in France.

The addition of important dates often appears to bring out subsequent dates of equal importance.

The following is a striking illustration from French history:

Revolution in France and fall of Robespierre took place in	1794
The numbers of this date added together give	21
The fall of Napoleon	1815
1815 added gives	15
Fall of Charles X and Revolution in France	1830
1830 added gives	12
Death of the King Louis Philippe	1842
1842 added gives	15
End of Crimean War	1857
1857 added gives	21
The famous Treaty of Berlin	1878
1878 added gives	24
Danger of War with England over Fashoda	1902
1902 added gives	12
World War I	1914
1914 added gives	15
A date which was another crisis in French history	1929

12

Some Additional Information

OUT OF THE MANY thousands of letters I have received, I shall now endeavour to answer those which appear to me as the most important.

'Should the words Mr., Mrs., or Miss be calculated when working out the complete number of a name?'

Answer: As I have explained before, it is *'the name one is most known by'* that should be used in working out the number of a name.

If, for example, a young lady is always addressed or spoken of as, say, Miss Jones—as is often the case in a large business etablishment—then in connection *with that business* in which she is employed, Miss Jones should certainly take that name as the one she is most known by and work out the number of the name 'Miss Jones' and use it, *but only in relation to the business she is employed in*. It is, in fact, her 'trade name;' but for her home life or her private affairs she should work out the Christian name she is called by or the 'pet' name she is known under. When the same young lady enters the state of matrimony and becomes 'Mrs.' she should then work out the numbers for her new title, but always keeping the numbers of her Christian or 'pet' name *for her home and private life*. The same rule applies to every woman known and called continually 'Mrs. Smith' or 'Mrs. Jones,' as the case may be, in the circle of friends or acquaintances in which she is called

'Mrs.'

Men in business for themselves or in large establishments, who are generally called 'Mr.' before their name, should also follow the above rule.

When a man or woman has many Christian names, they should only take the number made by the principal one—that they *are most known by*.

The same rule applies to every prefix or title a man or woman may obtain by *right of birth or as an honour*.

A good illustration of this is the case of the famous Melba.

The great diva's surname worked out to the compound number of 15, with 6 for the single, both being excellent for success. In one of my Press articles, speaking of the number 15, I said: 'If this number is associated with a good or fortunate single number, it can be very lucky and powerful. It is peculiarly associated with "good talkers" and often with gifts of eloquence, music, art and strong personal magnetism.' All these qualities were characteristic of the great Melba, as she was called all through her successful career.

Her signature, Nellie Melba, produces the number 10, also a fortunate number, and the single number 1, which is a number of strong individuality and ambition. It also denotes that people possessing this number have the desire to become the head or chief in whatever profession or occupation they take up·

If the number of her title, 'Dame,' which is the lucky number of 5, be added to the name Nellie Melba, the total of the last digits are: Dame 5, Nellie 4, Melba 6, giving again the compound number 15, so that as long as this famous woman existed good fortune always favoured her

I will now give an example of a title which produces

one of the unfortunate numbers, the curious effect it foreshadows as far as the promise of good luck is concerned.

In cases where the addition of the number of the title produces a 4 or an 8, it foreshadows that the fortunate numbers of the name have ceased their luck or power, and in such cases the title will become a detriment and not a happiness.

An illustration which may be given in connection with this is that of Napoleon. This name works out to the compound number of 41, which, as I state in my writings, is 'a magical number usually associated with combinations of peoples or nations.' The single number is a 5, also fortunate. When Napoleon became Emperor of France his name became Napoleon I, the 1 making his compound number 42 with the single number of 6. Both of these again are numbers of power and good fortune and he went down to posterity as the Great Napoleon.

In the case of Napoleon III the compound number becomes 44, which I stated in my articles 'is a number of the gravest warnings for the future; it foreshadows disasters brought about by association with others and bad advice'—exactly what happened to Napoleon III. Again, the single number of his name became an 8. Even the magic of the name Napoleon was overshadowed by it, and Napoleon III went down to posterity as 'the man who lost France.'

I think these illustrations will help to show how a prefix to a name, or a title acquired or inherited, fits in with this wonderful science of Numerology, and the number it gives added to the other numbers is a further indication of good or evil fortune for the future.

The title given to kings and queens when they ascend the throne, especially when taken in connection with their birth number, is generally very interesting.

In the case of King Edward VII, he changed his name when he came to the throne from Albert to Edward, the name he took working out as follows:

King.	11 =	2
Edward	22 =	4
VII	=	7
		13

I have described this number in a previous chapter as a number of warning with its strange symbolism of 'a skeleton' or 'death.'

It was certainly a warning of great changes that were about to occur in England, and taken in conjunction with his birth number, November 9th, by adding the 4 produced by the 13 to the 9, they again made a 13, which doubled the warning and also indicated a short reign.

13

How to Find the 'Lucky' Day

IN ANSWER TO MANY LETTERS, I take this opportunity of explaining a point of very great importance, namely, how to find the 'lucky' day.

I have stated that the birth number is the most important when the individual wants *to carry out his own plans*.

For example, a person we will say born on the 1st of a month will find *for all general purposes* that if he or she will use all dates making the Number One series, such as the 1st, 10th, 19th, or 28th of any month, especially during what is called the 'period of the 1' and 'the period of the 2,' namely, from June 21st to July 20th (period of the 2), and from July 21st to August 20th (period of the 1), they will have a far better chance of carrying out their plans successfully than if they did not follow this rule and did not know what dates to use for the best.

This is quite independent of any other rule, and I strongly recommend it.

To get a still more powerful vibration, I have advised that persons should try to make the number of their name (when they have worked out the letters of it by what is called the Mystic or Ancient Hebrew Alphabet) the same series as the number that is given by their birth date, and I have explained in a previous chapter how to do this by adding a letter to their name or taking away a letter, as the case may be. If these two numbers agree or are in harmony with one another, then they should use the date that is given to commence anything important, or endeavour to cary out their plans on that number which is indicated. They must, however, bear in mind that any number of the series they belong to is equally important.

Example

The person born on the 1st of the month will find the 10th, 19th, or 28th of equal importance to the number 1 on which they were born, and so on with every other birth number.

Naturally, when people begin to follow this idea, they must not expect to find their luck change in an instant, as if by magic. I have several letters before me as I write, where the writers expected their 'luck' to change for the better within twenty-four hours. There was one man who wrote that 'at the end of a week he had found no change in his bad luck,' but at the end of three months the same man again wrote to say that towards the middle of the third month he began to notice a distinct improvement in all his affairs.

Some of the writers have also apparently not grasped the example I gave in working out the number of the name of a man I called 'John Smith.' I stated in a previous chapter that if 'John Smith' wanted to find out a favourable date to ask his employer for an increase in his wages he should add the numbers given by the name 'John Smith' together, then add the single number of the date he wanted to know about and lastly to add his Birth number. The result was a total of 15 at the last compound number with 6 as the last single number. I said, 'Look up what I have given as the symbolism of the 15, and you will find it stated "for obtaining money, gifts, and favours from others it is a fortunate number," ' and therefore the date 'John Smith' wanted to see his employer would be a favourable date for him to make his request.

This was given only as an illustration of finding out if one particular date would be likely to be favourable *for that special purpose*, but I never intended this to be employed to the exclusion of the other definite rule for *continual action all through the year* on the series given by the Birth number, such as for a number 1 person to use all dates that make a 1, as the 1st, 10th, etc.

It will be noticed that in the latter case the rule is *individual or personal*; in the 'John Smith' case another life, namely the employer, was also concerned, and in consequence the rule given would not work out with such certainty.

14

Colours and Numbers

THERE IS NO REASON for anyone to get confused between the colours given by the number of the month and those given by the number of the day, if one will bear in mind that the number of the month is not as *close or intimate in its relationship to the individual* as is the colour indicated by the number of birth.

Take the month of January, for example. The 'period of the number 8' as set out in chapter 60 is from December 21st to January 20th *in its positive aspect*, and from January 21st to February 21st *in its negative aspect*. The number 8, as I stated, has for its colours 'all shades of dark grey, dark blue, and purple.' In the astrological section of this book I give the same colours with the addition of 'violet,' and under the heading of 'colours of the number 8' in the same section I have extended the list slightly by giving 'all tones of dark greys, blues, browns, and russet shades.' For the lucky jewels I have given 'all dark stones, such as dull rubies, carbuncles, and the deep-toned sapphire, which is most markedly the jewel of the number 8.' In the same section for persons born under a 4, I have given 'all shades of grey and fawn and electric shades and the minor tints of yellow and green.' In this work on numerology I have simply condensed the colours for the number 4 people to what are called 'half shades, half tones, or electric colours,' and have stated that 'electric blues and greys seem to suit them best of all. In all this there is no contradiction of terms, as the writers of many letters to me appear to imagine. There are so many sides to the study of the occult value of numbers that one cannot put all the information in one book.[1]

The following information will, I think, be useful, and I am giving it in order to clear up a point which I have noticed in many of the letters that have been received.

Namely: A person born on, say, January 6th will read in my astrological section that January is the 'period of the 8,' and that the colours for the number 8 are 'all tones of grey, all ranges of violet and purple, also black.' Many of those who have written to me are puzzled to know whether they should use the colours of the 8 or those belonging to the number 6. My answer is, *employ most decidedly in such a case* the colours of the number 6 as the principal, individual, and 'lucky' colours to use, but as the person was born in the 'period of the 8' he or she can use, if they wish, *but as secondary* colours, those given by the number 8.

Another illustration I will give is for those born in the 'period of the 9,' namely between March 21st to April 27th, which is *the positive period of the* 9, and those born *in its negative period*, namely, between October 21st and November 27th.

If one will look up the colours I have given earlier to the number 9, they will find that they are 'all shades of crimson or red, all rose tones and pink' for the *positive period*, while for the *negative period* in my astrological section if one reads about the period

---

[1] The deep-toned sapphire is also the principal jewel of the number 4, and all its series.

October-November, one will notice I say 'all shades of *crimson and* blue.'

Where does blue come in? one may ask.

Because *the opposite Sign of the Zodiac* to the period October 21st to November 27th is what is called *'the House of Venus'* in her positive aspect, and as Venus, which is also the number 6, represents in this wonderful colour scheme of Nature all shades of blue, these blue rays appear to cross from one side of the Zodiac to the other and so become a favourable colour for persons born in the *negative period of the nnmber* 9, as well as, 'all shades of crimson.'

Going back to the 'periods of the number 9' for a moment we find the basic colours for both these periods are red, crimson, and pink, but the same rule applies as it did in my example for the 'period of the 8.' A person born on a 6, such as on the 6th, 15th, or 24th *in the period of the* 9, would have as his or her *principal colour* all shades of blue, with red, crimson, or pink, as his or her *secondary colours*.

The same rule applies to every month in the year and to every date of birth. It is quite simple when one has once grasped this principle and can appreciate the marvellous harmony of this wonderful universe in which we live.

15

The Value of Concentration in Regard to One's Number

IN ORDER TO HELP my readers to make the best of whatever their number may be, I will now give advice which I am sure will be found of great assistance to those who want to try to make the most of their lives.

Once the principal or dominating number of the life has been found, then the next step is *to increase its power as much as possible*, the exception being those who are born under the 8, namely the 8th, 17th, or 28th of any month, to whom I will give advice on this point later.

This increase of power can be obtained by employing one of the *greatest forces* that man is endowed with, namely the Power of Concentration.

There are very few people who know anything about this extraordinary power.

All successful men and women are endowed with it, many use it unconsciously. Some are born with it, others develop it, but the majority of mankind do not use it at all.

One may often have noticed the feeble, 'wishy-washy' way most people talk. One may have tried hard to follow some rambling statement, but have found at the end that one hardly knows 'what it was all about,' or that the person who has tried to interest you has made no impression on you whatever. This has been due to the fact that the man or woman has no power of concentration, and consequently *no force behind their flow of words.*

It is the same when such people write a letter—again there may be a lot of words, even expressions and sentences well put together, but the letter has *no effect on you*, and very likely you toss it aside and think no more about it.

On the contrary, another person may say only a few words, but *those words take effect*; or they may write, and their sentences strike home—the secret of this mystery is *concentration of mind.*

The simplest way of developing this power is by the use of numbers. I will now explain.

The first thing to be done is to find one's own number, the birth number being in every case the simplest and the most certain; the next is to grasp *the meaning of that number*, and lastly, to think of oneself as if that number *belonged* to one, represented one, and were *part and parcel of one's aims and plans.*

This is the sure foundation on which to build.

We will now go a step further. The man or woman who has found his own distinct number should plan with firm determination to use that number in every way possible.

They should mentally look forward to the day or date when their number is to appear and plan that *on that day* they will take a certain course of action, and when that day or date arrives that they will go straight for what they want without shilly-shallying or hesitation of any kind.

Having read previous chapters on numbers, the reader has by now grasped the characteristics of other persons that are born under their own or other numbers. It is quite a simple matter to find out the day of the month on which the person one is going to interview was born, for if one does not ask the year of birth, even the woman most sensitive about her age will tell the date on which she was born.

A number 1 person will realise how useless it is to attempt to dominate a number 3 person. On the contrary, they must appeal to their ambition, their conscientiousness in carrying out their duties, their love of order and discipline, their sense of independence and the pride of honour and self that is the foundation principle of the number 3 person.

If they bear this in mind, *concentrating at the same time on their own plan* that made them seek the interview they will find that the number 3 person, instead of being difficult to approach, will, on the contrary, be willing to help and will most probably give ideas and suggestions that will be useful.

Having chosen a date for the interview on *one of their own numbers*, and by doing so, having concentrated their mind on this plan of action, they will find how easily they will be able to influence the person they have come to interview.

16

Combination Between 1 Hyphen 4 Persons and Numbers 4 and 8

FOLLOWING THE ILLUSTRATIONS I gave in the previous chapters on the usefulness of concentration on one's own number, so as to increase its power (except in case of those born under the 4 and 8), we will now take as an example a number 1 person meeting another of his own number. My readers have already learned from previous chapters that people born on the same series are naturally sympathetic to one another, and such knowledge gives the feeling in the first place that the other number 1 he is taking to is 'one of themselves,' as it were. This very sentiment radiating outwards destroys nervousness and allows the lines of human magnetism to vibrate in harmony from one to the other.

Let us now suppose that the number 1 person has arranged an interview with an individual born under the 2 series. In such a case he or she can select any date of the 1 or 2 series, such as the 1st, 2nd, 10th, 11th 19th, 20th, 28th, or 29th. The number 1 person has read that number 2 persons have the feminine qualities of the number 1, and that, though opposite in character, the vibrations of both 1 and 2 persons are harmonious, and that they make good combinations. With this knowledge in his possession the number 1 person will make the effort to combine with the ideas of number 2, and so happy and good results will be obtained.

A number 1 and a number 4 person will also meet on sympathetic and harmonious vibration for the reason that in Numerology the number 1 is always associated with the 4 and these numbers are written as 1 hyphen 4, and 4 hyphen 1, but as all number 4 persons have a very decided individuality, they must not be subjugated by the 1 person, but must be allowed to keep their own distinct character and to see things from their own point of view. If the number 1 person will keep the peculiar temperament of the number 4 in mind, any combination with a number 4 person should be most successful.

Behind all these ideas as far as success is concerned, as I have said at the commencement is the development of the power of concentration *on one's own number*, so as to *increase its influence*. This holds good for all the numbers except those born under the 4 and 8.

In previous chapters I have already warned all those under the 4's and 8's, such as the persons born on the 4th, 8th, 13th, 17th, 22nd, 26th, and 31st to avoid all numbers making an 8 or a 4 as much as possible; not to live in houses that have such numbers, and not to choose dates that make them.

In preceding pages I have gone into fuller details as to the 4 and 8 series, but briefly the rule for such persons to follow is: *Never increase the power of these numbers*. Consequently they must *not* follow the rule laid down for those born under the other numbers, but on the contrary they should do the very opposite.

As they cannot alter their Birth number, they can alter the number made by their name and cause it to produce one of the more fortunate series, especially one of a strong vibration such as a 1, 3, 5, or 6. Having definitely fixed in this way that they are going *to be represented* by the strong number they have made out of their name, they should then follow the rule I gave previously, namely, *think of themselves as that number* and do everything that is important on dates that make that number. If they do this, *and do it persistently*, the number 4 or 8 persons will get away from the bad luck such people generally experience and so become as equally fortunate as others.

They must not, however, expect the change to be seen in a few days, as so many in their impatience do, but in a reasonable space of time they will see very marked results in their favour.

17

More Information About Persons Born Under the Numbers 4 and 8

I HAVE RECEIVED so many letters from number 4 and 8 people, asking for advice, that I think it will be useful to devote an entire chapter to such cases.

Out of every hundred letters, eighty write testifying to the accuracy of my system of numbers, especially as regard the hard luck that appears to pursue persons who have the combination of 4 and 8 continually cropping up in their lives.

The 4 itself and all its series is not so much to be dreaded. Persons born on the 4th, 13th, 22nd, and 31st will find these dates and numbers the most important in their lives, but as the 4 in Numerology is always associated with the number 1, and in nearly all systems is written as 4 hyphen 1, or 1 hyphen 4, and as the 1 is a strong and powerful number, I advise the number 4 persons to use *the strong number* as much as possible and select all dates such as the 1st, 10th, 19th, and 28th for their most important efforts, and to endeavour to live in houses whose number or the addition of whose number makes a number 1. They should also remember that as what is called the interchangeable numbers of the 1 hyphen 4 series are the 2 hyphen 7 and all their series, they need not be afraid of such dates or numbers as the 2nd, 6th, 11th, 16th, 20th, 25th, or 29th.

It is only when the combination of the 4 and 8 are

continually cropping up that those born under such numbers should do their utmost to avoid them.

Example

A man born on either the 4th, 13th, 22nd, or 31st marries a woman born on either the 8th, 17th, or 26th. He will most certainly find that 4's and 8's will influence his life more than any other number, generally bringing sadness, ill-luck, or terrible blows of fate in their train. To this number 4 man or woman, I decidedly say avoid using all 4's and 8's and use the number 1 series instead, and for the next best use the 2 hyphen 7 series.

For some reason, due probably to some law of magnetic vibration, 4 and 8 people generally attract one another, but from *a purely worldly* standpoint the combination cannot be considered 'lucky.' They often show the highest devotion to one another during illness and misfortune, and some of the greatest examples of self-sacrifice are found when 4's and 8's marry or make a combination together.

Number 8 persons belong to a still more fatalistic law of vibration and appear to be 'children of fate' more than any other class.

They can be just as noble in character, as devoted and self-sacrificing as the best of their fellow mortals, but *they seldom get the reward that they are entitled to* If they rise in life to any high position it is generally one of grave responsibility, anxiety, and care. Such persons can become rich, but wealth seldom brings them happiness, and for love they are generally called on to pay too high a price.

My advice to them is: If they find the 4's and 8's continually coming into their lives and associated with sorrow, disappointment, ill-fate, and ill-luck, they should determinately avoid such numbers and all their series. They should, in such a case, so alter their name number, following the examples I have given in previous chapters, to produce one of the more fortunate series, such as a 1, 3, 5, or 6, and carry out their plans on dates that make these numbers. If they will do this they will completely alter their ill-luck and control as it were the curious fate that appears to follow them.

If, however, they prefer, as many do, to carry out the *full force and meaning of their number* 8, without caring what the worldly result may be, in that case they should do exactly as I have said for the other numbers and do everything important on dates and numbers that make the 8, such as the 8th, 17th, 26th, also the 4th, 13th, 22nd, and 31st.

If they do this they will be equally successful, but in leading peculiarly fatalistic lives, being, if I may use the expression, 'marked' people in whatever path of life they may make their own.

Many have written to ask how to change from an unlucky or fatalistic set of numbers to more fortunate ones. This question is generally asked by people who are born under the series of 4's and 8's, and who have proved, as I have said, that all combinations of such numbers have been more or less associated with fatalistic events in the life. In such cases, when persons are born on the 4th, 13th, 22nd, or 31st in any month they should try to avoid doing important things on dates making the 8 or any of its combinations, such as the 8th, 17th, 26th, and *take instead the number* 1 series, *or the number of the Zodiacal period of the month they are born in*. For example: A person born between February 19th and March 20th being in the 'period of the 3,' if they happen to be born on February 22nd or 26th or on March 4th, 8th, 13th, 17th, or 22nd, will find it more lucky for them to use the 3 series instead of their birth number, the 4 or 8. In fact, in such cases it will be better for them to drop the birth number altogether.

The same rule will apply to all the other month periods of the year with *the exception of the period* from December 21st to January 20th, the period of the number 8 positive, and from January 21st to February 19th, the period of number 8 negative. If born in these two periods the 4 and 8 people *must not select the number of the month period*, because if they did they would only increase the power of the 4 and 8. I advise them in such cases to take the number of the month period *exactly opposite to their Zodiac period*, which is: For December 21st to January 20th, the opposite numbers are those of June 21st to July 20th, which, if they refer to Chapter 2 of this book, they will find is the period of the 2—7. For people born January 21st to February 19th, the opposite period of the Zodiac is July 21st to August 20th, the numbers of which are 1—4. By following this rule all people who have the 4 and 8 for their birth number will be able to select numbers to use in place of the series of their 4's and 8's, and by employing the new numbers, will, in a short time, begin to notice how much more fortunate their lives have become.

They should employ also the colours and jewels which their *new numbers indicate* instead of those given for the 4's and 8's.

I feel sure this information will be useful to many hundreds who have asked questions on this extremely important point.

Many number 2 persons have written and asked me why it is that they find as well as their own number, the 2, 11, 20, and 29th, that the 8 appears to have a great importance in their lives. The reason for this is that the 8, being a very strong number, with a fatalistic tendency, tries to dominate the weaker number 2, which has a relation to itself as 4 times 2 is 8, but the 8 is not a happy combination when it comes into the lives of number 2 persons, and it should always be regarded as a warning of sorrow and disappointment or fatalistic experiences of some kind.

The 4 will also be found to have a great deal of influence with number 2 persons, but this is because it not only represents the double of the number 2, but it is also one of the interchangeable numbers, such as 1 and 4 are the interchangeable numbers of the 2 and 7.

18

The Affinity of Colours and Numbers
and
How Music and Numbers are Associated

NUMBER 1 PERSONS, namely those born on the 1st, 10th, 19th, or 28th (numbers which by the addition of themselves produce the number 1), should dress themselves as much as possible in all shades of brown (light or dark) and all shades of yellow or gold colours, or at least have some of these colours about their person. If they have the freedom to select colours for their sleeping rooms, they should follow the same rule.

They will find this colour rule will have an excellent effect in soothing their nerves, and they will rest and sleep better in rooms having their own colours.

Number 2 persons, namely, those born on the 2nd, 11th, 20th, or 29th, should wear all shades of green from the darkest to the lightest shade, also cream and white.

They should avoid all heavy dark colours, especially black, purple, and dark red.

Number 3 persons, namely, those born on the 3rd, 12th, 21st, or 30th, should wear shades of mauve, violet, or the pale or lilac shades of purple, but as men cannot easily dress in such colours, they should at least employ them in the neckties, shirts, or handkerchiefs.

Number 4 persons, namely, those born on the 4th, 13th, 22nd, or 31st, should wear what are called the 'electric colours,' blue, greys, electric blues, and what are known as 'half shades.' They should avoid strong or positive colours of all kinds.

Number 5 persons, namely, those born on the 5th, 14th, or 23rd, should wear the light shades of all colours especially light greys, white, and glistening materials.

They should never wear dark colours if they can possibly avoid doing so.

Number 6 persons, namely, those born on the 6th, 15th, or 24th, should wear all shades of blue, from the lightest to the dark navy, what is known as the full or real blue, not 'electric blue.' For secondary colours, they can also wear shades of rose or pink, but not red, scarlet, or crimson, unless they are born between March 28st to April 24th, or between October 21st to November 24th.

Number 7 persons, namely, those born on the 7th, 16th, or 25th should, like the number 2 persons were all shades of pale green, white, yellow, and gold colours. The palest possible shades are best for them, such as what are know as 'pastel shades.'

Number 8 persons, namely, those born on the 8th, 17th, or 26th, should wear all shades of dark grey, dark blue, purple, and black; light and gaudy colours are out of place with them and should be avoided.

Number 9 persons, namely, those born on the 9th, 18th, or 27th, should wear all shades of red, rose, crimson, pink, or red purple. The darker or rich shades of these colours are best for them.

Red is the colour of the soldier, the colour of energy, restlessness and revolution. It is the chosen colour of the Revolutionist and Anarchist; hence, the origin of the 'red flag.'

On account of the magnetic rays sent off by a

number 9 person, their presence often irritates people belonging to other numbers, except those born under the number 1, the 3, the 5, the 6, or their own number. People born under the other numbers are very often nervous or uncomfortable in the presence of a number 9 person.

Numbers and music show very decided affinities. The number 1, 3, and 9 persons like martial, inspiring, or what may be called 'full-blooded' tones; number 2 and 7 persons are more partial to string and wind instruments, such as the violin,' cello, harp, pipes, etc.; number 6 persons like romatic, sweet music of all kinds with a lilt and rhythm; number 5 persons lean towards either extremely original or unusual music, something off the beaten track. Number 4 and 8 persons, if musical, have a special leaning for the organ and make magnificent choir or choral leaders, but in all their music there is an undertone of plaintiveness, melancholy, religious fervour, or fatalism.

The following are a few examples of countries having their own individual or what is called National Music, in accordance with the planet and number by which they are governed.

England and Germany, governed by Mars (number 9), martial, inspiring, or 'full-blooded' music.

The United States, governed by the Planet Mercury (number 5), can use the qualities of that number and adapt itself to all types of music, but will always lean to what is original, new, and out of the ordinary—hence this country is the natural birthplace of what is called 'jazz' or syncopated music.

19

Numbers and Disease: Planetary Significance of Herbal Cures

IN SOME PRESS ARTICLES I gave an account of the various diseases that are associated with persons born under the numbers that make their birth date. I have received so many letters testifying to the accuracy of this system and begging me to give further information as to indications from occultism regarding the cure of diseases, that I have much pleasure in giving in this chapter the name of herbs that are beneficial to persons born under the different numbers.

I have collected this information from some of the most ancient sources of knowledge on occultism and from those who have devoted their lives to investigation of the subject. To this I have added my own life-long experience, in the belief that by the study of Nature we may find the secrets of Nature.

Number 1 persons, or all those born on the 1st, 10th, 19th, and 28th, of any month, have a tendency to suffer from the heart in some form or another, such as palpitation, irregular circulation, and in advanced life, high blood-pressure. They are also likely to have trouble with the eyes, or astigmatism, and would do well to have their sight carefully tested from time to time.

The principal herbs and fruits for number 1 persons, or all those whose birth number is the 1st, 10th,

19th, or 28th, are:

Raisins, camomile, eye-bright, St. John's wort, saffron, cloves, nutmeg, sorrel, borage, gentian root, lavender, bay leaves, oranges, lemons, dates, thyme, myrrh, musk vervain, ginger, barley (barley bread and barley water). Number 1 persons should eat honey as much as possible.

They will find their nineteenth, twenty-eighth, thirty-seventh, and fifty-fifth years will bring them important changes in health one way or the other.

The months to most guarded against for ill-health and overwork are: October, December, and January.

Number 2 persons, or all those whose birth number is the 2nd, 11th, 20th, or 29th, have a tendency to suffer with the stomach and digestive organs.

The principal herbs for number 2 persons, or those born on the 2nd, 11th, 20th, or 29th of any month, are: Lettuce, cabbages, turnips, cucumber, melon, chicory or endive, rapeseed, colewort, moonwort, linseed, water plantain, and ash of willow.

They will find the twentieth, twenty-fifth, twenty-ninth, forty-third, forty-seventh, fifty-second, and sixty-fifth years will bring them important changes in health. The three months to be most guarded against for ill-health and overwork are January, February, and July.

Number 3 persons, or all those born on the 3rd, 12th, 21st, or 30th, have a tendency to suffer from overstrain of the nervous system, generally brought on by overwork and their desire not to spare themselves in any thing they do.

They are inclined to have attacks of neuritis and sciatica, also many forms of skin troubles.

The principal herbs for number 3 persons, or those born on the 3rd, 12th, or 30th of any month, are beets, borage, bilberries, asparagus, dandelion, endive, ewerwort, lungwort, sage, cherries, barberries, strawberries, apples, mulberries, peaches, olives, rhubarb, gooseberries pomegranates, pineapples, grapes, mint, saffron, nutmegs, cloves, sweet marjoram, St. John's wort, almonds, figs, hazel-nuts, and wheat.

The months to be most guarded against for ill-health and overwork are December, February, June, and September. The important years for changes in health are the twelfth, twenty-first, thirty-ninth, forty-eighth, and fifty-seventh.

Number 4 persons, or all those born on the 4th, 13th, 22nd, or 31st, have a likelihood of suffering from mysterious ailments, difficult of ordinary diagnosis. They are more or less inclined to melancholia, anaemia and pains in the head and back.

The principal herbs for number 4 persons, or those born on the 4th, 13th, 22nd, or 31st of any month, are spinach, sage, pilewort, wintergreen, medlars, icelandmoss, and Solomon's seal. Number 4 persons derive the greatest benefit from electric treatment of all kinds, mental suggestion, and hypnotism. They should be particularly careful to avoid drugs, also highly seasoned dishes and red meat.

The months to be guarded against for ill-health and overwork are January, February, July, August, and September.

The important years for their health are the thirteenth, twenty-second, thirty-first, fortieth, forty-ninth, and fifty-eighth.

Number 5 persons, or all those born on the 5th, 14th, or 23rd, have a tendency to overstrain the nervous system. They are inclined to attempt too much mentally, to live too much on their nerves. They are likely to bring on such things as neuritis and are prone to nervous prostration and insomnia. Sleep, rest, and quietude are the best medicines they can employ.

The principal herbs for number 5 persons or those born on the 5th, 14th, or 23rd of any month, are carrots, parsnips, sea-kale, oats in the from of oatmeal or bread, parsley, sweet marjoram, champignons, caraway seeds, thyme, nuts of all kinds, but especially hazel-nuts and walnuts.

The months to be most guarded against for ill-health and overwork are June, September, and December.

The important years for changes in their health are the fourteenth, twenty-third, forty-first, and fiftieth years.

Number 6 persons, or all those born on the 6th, 15th, or 24th, are inclined to suffer with the throat, nose, and upper part of the lungs. As a rule they have a strong robust constitution, especially if they can live in the open or in the country, where they can have plenty of air and exercise. Women born under the number 6 often suffer with their breasts. The heart as a general rule becomes affected in the latter years and produces irregular circulation of the blood.

The herbs for number 6 persons, or those born on the 6th, 15th, or 24th of any month, are all kinds of beans, parsnips, spinach, marrows, mint, melons motherwort, pomegranates, apples, peaches, apricots, figs, walnuts, almonds and the juice of maidenhair-fern, daffodils, wild thyme, musk, violets, vervain, and rose leaves.

The months to be most guarded against for ill-health and overwork are May, October, and November.

They will find that the fifteenth, twenty-fourth, forty-second, fifty-first, and sixtieth years will bring them important changes in health.

Number 7 persons, or those who are born on the

7th, 16th, or 25th, are more easily affected by worry and annoyance than any other class. As long as things are going smoothly, they can get through any amount of work, but if worried, either by circumstances or people, they are inclined to imagine things are worse than they are and get easily despondent and melancholy.

They are extremely sensitive to their surroundings; they will gladly accept any responsibility for those who appear to appreciate them; they are unusually conscientious in doing any work that is interesting to them, but as they are stronger mentally than physically, they have often frail bodies that attempt too much for their strength. They are inclined to have some peculiar delicacy in connection with the skin; it is either extremely sensitive to friction, or has some peculiarity as regards perspiration.

The principal herbs for number 7 persons, or those born on the 7th, 16th, or 25th in any month, are lettuce, cabbage, chicory or endive, cucumber, colewort, linseed, mushrooms, ceps, sorrel, apples, grapes, and the juices of all fruits. The months to be most guarded against for ill-health and overwork are January, February, July and August.

The most important years for changes in health are the seventh, sixteenth, twenty-fifth, thirty-fourth, forty-third, fifty-second, and sixty-first.

Number 8 persons, or those born on the 8th, 17th, or 26th, are as a rule liable to trouble with the liver, bile and intestines. They are prone to suffer with headaches and rheumatism. They should avoid animal food as much as possible and live on fruit, herbs, and vegetables.

The principal herbs for number 8 persons, or those born on the 8th, 17th, or 26th in any month, are spinach, winter green, angelica, wild carrot, marshmallow, plantain, sage, pilewort, ragwort, shepherd's purse, Solomon's seal, vervain, elder flowers, gravel root, mandrake root, celery.

The months to be most guarded against for ill-health and effects of overwork are December, January, February and July. They will find the most important years for changes in health are the seventeenth, twenty-sixth, thirty-fifth, forty-fourth, fifty-third, and sixty-second.

Number 9 persons, or those born on the 9th, 18th, or 27th, are more or less inclined to fevers of all kinds, measles, chicken-pox, scarlatina, and such-like. They should avoid rich food, also alcoholic drinks or wines.

The principal herbs for number 9 persons, or those born on the 9th, 18th, or 27th of any month, are onions, garlic leeks, horse-radish, rhubarb, mustard-seed, wormwood, betony, spear-wort, white hellebore, ginger pepper, broom, rape, madder, hops, danewort, and juice of nettles.

The months to be most guarded against for ill-health or the effects of overwork are April, May, October, and November.

The will find the most important years for changes in the health are the ninth, eighteenth, twenty-seventh, thirty-sixth, forty-fifth, and sixty-third.

The herbs that have been mentioned in these pages can be obtained from all good herbalists in almost all countries. Herbs are Nature's own remedies.

20

How to Know What City, Town or Place is Fortune for One to Live in

IN THIS CHAPTER I intend to show how each person may more easily find if any city, town, or place is in a harmonious vibration with themselves.

Such information should be of great value to those who find, as so many do, that a certain town or place has proved unfortunate; they may desire to make a change, but as they have nothing to guide them, they do not know what to do or how to arrive at decision. The following rules will, I believe, be of great help to all such people.

Taking the numbers 1 to 9 as the foundation numbers, which by now all those readers who have followed this book will know are the basic numbers by which all calculation on this earth is founded, I will therefore give examples of how each birth number may be found in any city, town, or place.

Work out the numbers of the name of the city or town by the numbers given to eaeh letter by the Mystic Alphabet which I give in Chapter 3. Put these numbers under each letter and add them together until only one figure remains; if this single number corresponds to the birth number, then the vibrations of that city, town, or place will accordt with the individual, and the district indicated by the number should be fortunate for the person whose birth number corresponds with it, and still more so if the person's name number is also in accord.

Number 1 persons, such as all those born on the 1st, 10th, 19th, or 28th, would therefore find the following towns more likely to be favourable. We will take as an example Manchester. The name works out as follows:

MANCHESTER
4 1 5 3 5 5 3 4 5 2 = 37 and 3 plus 7
= 10 or the single number 1.

Other towns that make the number 1 are:

Birmingham	1
Boston	1
New York	1
Alexandria	1
Whitechapel	1

or any other town or place that will by this system produce the number 1.

Number 1 and 4 and number 2 and 7 persons have a greater choice than those born under any of the other numbers, for, as I have previously explained in my chapters on this subject, number 1 belongs to the 1 hyphen 4 series whose interchangeable or sympathetic numbers are the 2 hyphen 7 series, therefore number 1, 2, 4, or 7 persons could select all places that give as their single number any of the series of 1, 2, 4, or 7.

Number 2 persons, or all those born on the 2nd, 11th, 20th, or 29th, can select any town whose final number makes any one of the above series, but more especially a town making their own series of the 2. We will take as an example:

LEEDS
3 5 5 4 3 = 20 = 2

or any of the following places which all total to the number 2:

Plymouth	2
Los Angeles	2
Norwich	2
Brighton	2

Number 3 persons, or all those born on the 3rd, 12th, 21st, or 30th, can take as an example:

CREWE
2 3 5 6 5 = 21 = 3

or any of the following towns which add to the number 3, such as:

Dublin	3
Bath	3
Reading	3
Limerick	3
Moscow	3
Melbourne	3
York	3
Nottingham	3
Devonport	3
Bradford	3

Number 4 persons, or all those born on the 4th, 13th, 22nd, or 31st, can take as an example:

LONDON
3 7 5 4 7 5 = 31 = 4

or any of the following towns which add to the number 4, such as:

Paisley	4
Bristol	4
Leicester	4
Quebec	4
Montreal	4
Stockport	4
Salisbury	4

or any town indicated by the numbers of the 1, 2, 4, or 7 series, as I explained earlier.

Number 5 persons, or all those born on the 5th, 14th, or 23rd, can take as an example:

TAUNTON
4 1 6 5 4 7 5 = 32 = 5

or any of the following towns which add to the number 5, such as:

Southport	5
Portsmouth	5
Chicago	5
Cork	5
Vienna	5

But as the number 5 is the only number that can associate or harmonise with any other number, they need not be so careful as to what place they select, for as they can get on with persons born under any other number almost equally as well as with those born under their own, so in the same way they get on equally well in any city or place no matter what its number may be.

Number 6 persons, or all those born on the 6th, 15th, or 24th, can take as an example:

LIVERPOOL
3 1 6 5 2 8 7 7 3 = 42 = 6

or any of the following towns, which add to the number 6, such as:

Edinburgh	6
Swansea	6
Paris	6
Dover	6
Worthing	6
Halifax	6
Oxford	6
Cologne	6
San Francisco	6
Cowes	6
Sheffield	6

Number 7 persons, or all those born on the 7th. 16th, or 25th, can take as an example:

W I G A N
6 1 3 1 5 = 16 = 7

or any of the following towns which add to the number 7, such as:

Doncaster	7
Hollywood	7
Whitehaven	7
Auckland	7
Calcutta	7
Tiverton	7
Grimsby	7
Preston	7

or any town indicated by the numbers of the 1, 2, 4, 7 series, as I explained earlier.

Number 8 persons, or all those born on the 8th, 17th, or 26th, can take as an example:

GLASGOW
3 3 1 3 3 7 6 = 26 = 8

or any of the following, such as:

Belfast	8
Stoke-on-Trent	8
Hull	8
Bombay	8
Bournemouth	8

But, as I have explained, I advise all number 4 and 8 persons not to increase the influence of the number 8 by employing or living under this strangely fatalistic number, but instead to make their name number work out to a more fortunate vibration, such as those of the 1, 3, 5, or 6 series.

Number 9 persons, or all those born on the 9th, 18th, or 27th, can take as an example:

WOLVERHAMPTON
6 7 3 6 5 2 5 1 4 8 4 7 5 = 63 = 9

or any of the following towns which add to the number 9, such as:

Blackpool	9
Whitehead	9
St. Louis	9
Berlin	9
Rome	9
Toronto	9
Brussels	9

As I have explained previously, the series of 3, 6, 9, if added together in any direction, produce a 9 as their final digit, so the persons born under any one of these series will find others born under any of these series sympathetic to them, so also can they take any city or town whose final number makes a 3, 6, 9, as if they used only their own individual number.

In conclusion, it should be borne in mind that towns and places should be regarded as the *larger octave of harmony*, the number of one's house *the more intimate*, the number of the date and day of the week *the more immediate as regards events*, and the birth number of persons in relation to oneself as *the more personal* as regards our feelings, affections, and home life.

If this is borne in mind, the reason and logic of this special system of Numerology is easily seen, and the harmony it makes for becomes apparent to every student of humanity.

21

Horse-Racing and Numbers

I HAVE RECEIVED so many letters asking for information as to how my system of numbers could be employed in 'betting,' that I cannot conclude this book without trying to give some advice on a subject that is of interest to so many thousands.

There is no doubt that the study of numbers can open up a new field for the successful backing of horses, but there is no saying more true than 'a little knowledge is a dangerous thing.'

My experience is that people are too much inclined to think that because they have proved that the system I teach has such a bearing on the leading events in their own individual lives, that without more preparation they are ready to plunge into racing and back any horse whose name makes the same number as their own.

The point so many people seem to forget is that horse-racing is an extremely complicated business, so much so that 'tips,' even from owners and jockeys, are as a rule as equally unreliable as the hundred and one systems that are offered daily to the public by almost every newspaper that one picks up.

Many important racing events have upset all theories as to forecasting the winner by a study of 'form,' previous running, and so forth. At many races complete outsiders have, for no apparent reason, beaten the most heavily backed favourites.

Can the study of numbers be used to give a clear indication of which horses are likely to be first, second, and third?

I say most emphatically that it can, but the trouble is that it is so rare to find persons who can 'keep their heads' when it comes to such a thing as a *systematic employment of any method*, and more particularly with numbers.

If one really made up one's mind to experiment with the system of numbers as set out in these pages in connection with betting, one would have to do it on the following lines:

To attend the race meeting in person.

Select a day whose number accords with one's own,

If possible, find out the jockeys whose birth number is the same as the number of the day.

When all these numbers are in accord, say, for example, if they all worked out to a number, such as the 9, then such horses, if they run under the numbers 9, 18, and 27 on that day would certainly be more likely to come in as first, second, and third than any others.

In such a case it would be necessary to back the three horses that are to run under the numbers, 9, 18, and 27 on the starting board for 'win and place,' If there were a greater number than 36 running in the race it would be necessary also to take in the horse under that number, but if too much money would be at stake by backing all four, a good rule is to select *the two youngest horses* out of the four and back these two for 'win and place.' If there were not much difference in age, the next rule to employ is to select *the youngest male horse* in preference to *the youngest female*.

22

Examples from the Names of Some Presidents of the United States

George Washington
IN taking illustrations from the names of Presidents of the United States, I cannot do better than start with the name of George Washington.

```
  G E O R G E        W A S H I N G T O N
  3 ·5 7 2 3 5       6 1 3 5 1 5 3 4 7 5
  ─────────          ───────────────────
     2 5                    4 0

     7                       4      =11=2
```

The number of the famous name of George Washington, the 1st President of the United States, worked out by the Chaldean or Hebrew alphabet, as set out in the example on Lloyd George, gives to the name GEORGE the compound number of 25, with its single of final digit of 7. On looking up the meaning of the compound number of 25 in chapter 4, it will be found stated :

> This is a number denoting strength gained through experience and benefits obtained through observation of people and things. It is not deemed exactly 'lucky,' as its success is given through strife and trials in the earlier life. It is favourable when it appears in regard to the future.

The word WASHINGTON works out to the compound number of 40, with its single digit of 4.

The meaning of this compound number is given in chapter 4 as :

> This is a number of thoughtful deduction, retrospection, and mental superiority over one's fellows, but, as it seems to belong to the mental plane, the persons it represents are likely to put all material things on one side—not because they have to, but because they wish to do so.

This is remarkably borne out by Washington's resignation of the position of Commander-in-Chief of the victorious American Army when he met his assembled Generals for the last time. His own words were, 'With heart full of love and gratitude, I now take leave of you.' Addressing the President of Congress, Washington said :

> The great events on which my resignation depended having, at length, taken place, I have now the honour to surrender into their [Congress's] hands the trust committed to me and to claim the indulgence of retiring from the service of my country. Having now finished the work assigned me, I retire.

This really great man, so justly called the 'Father of the United States,' refused to accept any reward for his long years of arduous sevice, and thus retired to his home at Mount Vernon.

The distinguished name of George Washington bears out in a remarkable manner the occult meaning of the numbers of this name.

If the final digits of 7 for GEORGE and 4 for WASHINGTON be added together they produce eleven

(1·1), with the single digit of 2. This compound number 11, on being raised to its higher octave, 20, gives for this compound number (see chapter 4) the symbol of 'The Awakening,' also 'The Judgment,' with the interpretation.

The awakening of new purpose, new plans, new ambitions, the call to action, but for some great purpose, cause, or duty.

It will thus be seen from this example how wonderfully this system of Numerology fits in with and explains the underlying qualities of the character of George Washington.

By knowing the birth date of an individual and seeing if the number of the date is in harmonious vibration with the number given by the name is of considerable help in arriving at a summing up of the general characteristics.

If the number of the birth date and the number given by the name are not in accord, the promise of the man's or woman's career will not be so definite.

Returning to the name of George Washington, as an example, the last digit is the figure 2, with 7 and 4 as the principal digits of the name.

Now, Washington's birthday is celebrated as February 22nd, which makes the double figure in this system to be written as 4 hyphen 1, with its interchangeable numbers of 2 hyphen 7. (See chapter 2.) Some people claim that his birth date was February 11th, in the old-style calendar. Should this be the date taken, it would not alter the affect of the number of his name working out to the final digit of a 2, because, whether it was February 22nd, a 4, or February 11th, a 2, they are both interchangeable numbers with one another, and in consequence the number of the name and the number of the birth date *are in harmonious vibration together.*

Should the number of the name and the number of the birth date not be in harmony or accord, it indicates that one is likely to find a jumble or unevenness in the plans and careers of the man or woman the numbers not in vibration to one another represent.

Abraham Lincoln

Abraham Lincoln born February 12th, 1809, assassinated on the night of Friday, April 14th, 1865, died April 15th.

The name works out as follows :

```
A B R A H A M        L I N C O L N
1 2 2 1 5 1 4        3 1 5 3 7 3 5
─────────────        ─────────────
     1 6                   2 7
     ──                    ──
     7                     9     = 16 = 7
```

In this case the birth number, the single digit 3, and the single digit of the name are not in harmonious accord.

The single digit of 3 for the birth is a powerful number, being in itself representative of the Planet Jupiter; it indicates underlying ambition, the power to rule and dictate. In describing these persons in chapter 55, I have stated :

Number 3 people...are decidedly ambitious; they are never satisfied in being in subordinate positions; their aim is to rise in the world, to have control and authority over others. They are excellent in the execution of commands; they love order and discipline in all things; they readily obey orders themselves, but they also insist on having their orders obeyed. Number 3 people often rise to the very highest positions in any business, profession, or sphere in which they may be found. They often excel in positions of authority in the army and navy, in government, and in life generally; and especially in all posts of trust and responsibility, as they are extremely conscientious in carrying out their duties.

The final digit of the name ABRAHAM LINCOLN, a 7, is more weak or gentle in its qualities, as I have stated in chapter 2 :

People born under the number 7...are very independent, original, and have strongly marked individuality...but in everything they do, they sooner or later show a peculiar philosophical outlook on life that tinges all their work.

I further said, number 7 people have 'a peculiar magnetism that has great influence over others.'

The description by this system of Numerology, it must be admitted, accords closely with the well-known character of Abraham Lincoln.

Turning to the more mysterious or hidden influences indicated by the compound numbers, if we add the single digit of the birth number, the 3, to the digit of the name number, the 7 they produce the compound number of 10. In chapter 4 we read :

10. Symbolised as the 'Wheel of Fortune.' It is a number of honour, of faith and self-confidence, of rise and fall; one's name will be known for good or evil, according to one's desires; it is fortunate number in the sense that one's plans are likely to be carried out.

Taking the compound number of the birth, February 12th, for another indication of the occult influences governing this career, we read for this number in chapter 4 :

12. The symbolism of this number is suffering

and anxiety, of mind. It is also indicated as 'the Sacrifice' or 'the Victim' and generally foreshadows one being sacrificed for the plans or intrigues of others.

Now, turning to the compound number of the name 16, we read in the same chapter :

> 16. This number has a most peculiar occult symbolism. It is pictured by 'a Tower Struck by Lightning from which a man is falling with a Crown on his head.' It is also called 'the Shattered Citadel.'
>
> It gives warning of some strange fatality awaiting one.

When one considers Lincoln's sudden assassination as he sat in a box in a theatre on the night of Friday, April 14th, one cannot help being astonished at the truth underlying this system of occult significance of the compound numbers.

Further, Abraham Lincoln was the 16th President of the United, the single digit of this number, the 7, corresponding to the single digit of his name.

Franklin Delano Roosevelt

Franklin Delano Roosevelt, the 32nd President of the United States, was born at Hyde Park, New York, at 8.18 p.m., January 30th, 1882.

The numbers made by his name are as follows :

```
F R A N K L I N        D E L A N O
8 2 1 5 2 3 1 5        4 5 3 1 5 7
———————————            ———————————
     2 7                    2 5
    ———                    ———
      9                      7
```

23

The Bible and Numbers

IN AN EARLIER CHAPTER of this book, I have given illustrations of the influence of the number 7 and other numbers in connection with the Hebrew race.

One of the great wonders of the world has been the fact that, in spite of privations and persecutions such as no other race ever endured, the Jewish people have held to their religion as set out in the pages of the volume of the Sacred Law, and furthermore, that this volume has become *the base of all law in every land and clime into which it has permeated.*

In this book, generally called the Bible, more knowledge is at times concealed than is revealed to the ordinary reader.

It may not have been noticed before, by the many people who have read the Bible through from cover to cover, that both *the shortest* and the *longest chapters* of this wonderful book are placed *in close proximity to each other*, the shortest being the 117th and the longest the 119th Psalm. Now the one intermediary chapter between the shortest and the longest, the 118th, presents in itself such a number of remarkable coincidences that one is forced to the conclusion that these three psalms *were purposely planned* to come together for a definite reason—that reason evidently being that the relation of such coincidences would sooner or later strike some searcher of truth, as an illustration of Divine Design and consequently proof of the Divine Inspiration that guided not only the writer of the Psalms, but thousands of years later *the translators of this book into other languages*.

The 118th Psalm, occupying as it does the remarkable position of being between the shortest and longest chapters of the Bible, actually contains *the middle or central verse of the entire Bible*. This, the middle verse of the Sacred Book, is the 8th verse of the 118th Psalm.[1]

Its words are significant in their meaning—they are an epitome of the great truth taught all through the preceding chapters or those that follow: 'It is better to trust in the Lord than to put confidence in man.'

Further, if one writes down in figures Psalm 118, verse 8, and puts these numbers side by side, they become 1188, which is the *exact number of chapters in the Bible*, besides the one that contains the remarkable verse above quoted and which, as I called attention to before, *is the middle verse of the entire book*.

Next to this 118th Psalm, the 117th stands out as the shortest chapter of the Bible, and not only is this a curious fact, but it is still doubly so, by being at the same time *the central chapter of* the Book, having exactly *as many chapters before it as after it*.

The most accurate way of finding out if the 117th Psalm is the central chapter of the Bible is to refer to the table usually printed in the beginning of the Authorised Version. This table contains six columns or 39 books of the Old Testament and 27 books of the New.

---

[1] The actual form and division of the Bible is the work of different minds, widely separated by time, by countries, and by training. There can therefore be no question of collusion in the carrying out of the evident design that underlies the construction of the Bible.

By adding together the numbers of chapters given by those six columns we get the number 1189, the total number of the chapters in the Bible, the middle one must therefore be the 595th, as there cannot be anything else than 594 chapters before it and 594 following it.

The very number of 595, which is the number of the 117th Psalm, calculated as a chapter of the Bible, conveys in itself the idea of perfect symmetry, namely it can be read the same whether from left to right, or vice versa; it represents in itself *the principle of perfect equilibrium* which consists of equal disposition of the parts of both sides of a centre.

This, the shortest chapter in the Bible and the central one of the entire Book, has a striking significance of its own:

"O praise the Lord all ye nations; praise Him all ye people. For His merciful kindness is great towards us; and the truth of the Lord endureth for ever."

One should not regard the extraordinary examples I have set out in these pages as isolated cases of mere coincidence, for when taken together, as they were evidently intended to be, they give the key to the construction of the Bible itself as a marvellous example of Divine inspiration. They tend to show that these three Psalms must have been written with a plan of forming these coincidences for some given purpose, and that the division and numeration of the entire Bible, so perfect in every way, *was prearranged* before even the greater part of it had been written by those who lived in later ages.

24

Astrology and Astrological Numbers

TO MANY PEOPLE the word Astrology merely stands for one of the many doubtful superstitious practices which come down to us from past ages; whereas, in fact, Astrology is the mathematical application of proved laws — laws which are no less valid than those of the complementary sciences of Palmistry and Numerology.

All sciences rest upon a very simple basis. Facts are painstakingly collected, experiments are based thereon, and deductions are made from the collected data. This same process obtains in chemistry, physics, biology and all other sciences. Once a given "law" has been established, the chemist is able to "predict" — if you like to put it that way — just what will happen in a given instance. The Astrologer works upon *exactly the same method*. He and his kind have found that if, for instance, the planet Mars be near the eastern horizon at the *exact* time and place of birth, the individual then born will be muscular, headstrong, combative, energetic. In other words, certain known phenomena in the heavens are coincident with, or related to, certain corresponding phenomena on the earth.

How, or why this should be, is not known. The simple facts remain, and can be proved by anybody with a little mathematical and astrological knowledge, and an "Ephemeris" for their year of birth. *The basic facts of Astrology have never been disproved.* But it must be remembered that the predictions made by the Astrologer are no more "occult" than the chemist's experiment previously related. Both are based on the assumption that "Law rules the Universe," an assumption universally accepted.

It is claimed by the student of Astrology that as regards the individual human being there is a connection between that which is born and the planets at the time, hence much can be learned from the heavens concerning the individual.

All living mankind can be grouped into twelve great classes, according to the month[1] in which they were born. True, widely different folk are born in one and the same month. But if twenty people born (say) between the 1st and 20th of January were analysed carefully, it would be found that, however different their superficial characteristics, they were all of similar mould, similar deep down at heart. Under the veneer due to their education, environment, social position, degree of mental development, etc., they would have certain basic and common qualities in common.

I have therefore gathered up the fruits of much observation and experience, and incorporated them in a series of Readings for the various months on the following pages. These generalities of character and fortune will be found, in the main, uncannily accurate. The descriptions will not cover all the qualities of every individual, and may at times be wrong in detail. Allowing for this inevitable percentage of error due to the individual case they will be found a reliable guide.

---

[1] Note that the Astrological "month" begins about the 21st of each calender month and runs to about the 21st of the next calendar month.

The finer shades of character, the manifestation of genius, special ability, abnormal or subnormal qualities of mind or emotional nature, can be judged only from the individual horoscope. This depends upon the hour, date and place of birth of the individual concerned. The erection and judgment of a horoscope involves recourse to personal study or a professional Astrologer.

Concerning the Moon
From the dawn of history the moon has played a most important part in the life of the human race. Her changing orb has served as a time-measure, an infallible calendar in Nature, ever since men have intelligently marked the flight of time.

Reference to the Bible, or the sacred books of all times and nations, reveals the importance attached to the Lunar phases in ceremonial religion. The movable feasts of our own Church depend year by year upon the Lunar Phases.

We know that at the Full Moon animals, birds and reptiles are very much more on the move than they are during the rest of the moon's alternation.

We know well enough that the ebb and flow of the tides is partly due to the pull of the moon—wherever "men go down to the sea in ships" they must heed her times and seasons.

We know of the traditional connection between the conditions of the mentally unstable and the moon's changes.

We know of the peculiar hallucinations which are produced by exposure to tropical moonlight during sleep.

We can trace the obvious and absolute correspondence between certain feminine functions and the

Lunar cycle of twenty-eight days.

Men who have studied natural phenomena in every age have credited the moon with an influence upon vegetable life, upon animal function, upon psychic activity in human beings.

The theories of the old-time alchemists have survived many centuries of materialism, to be finally rediscovered and proved true in essentials by the modern chemist and physicist. In the same way, the teachings of the old time Astrologers concerning Lunar influence (though they are loosely stated and mixed with much speculative dross) will be re-established by the enlightened Science of tomorrow.

At the moment we are concerned with the significance of the Lunar influence, and Lunar phases, *in everyday life*.

Let us briefly summarise the Astrological tradition:

All nature is assumed to be in a state of vibration, alternation, pulsation. In the human body, the muscles of the heart alternately contract and expand, pumping blood from the veins and forcing it through the arteries. The lungs inhale and exhale. The man wakes and sleeps, works and rests Winter follows summer. The very poles swing round in an age-long cycle.

Now, in a sense, the changing moon at once symbolises and presides over the various pulsations in the life activity of the globe on which we live—the earth.

This pulsation, or ebb and flow of the life currents of the earth, occurs more or less every thirty days. The outward or positive pulsation occurs during the fourteen to fifteen days when the moon is *increasing in light*—i.e., from the time of the New Moon to the time of the Full Moon. The compensating or negative pulsation is set up *by the moon's decrease*—from the

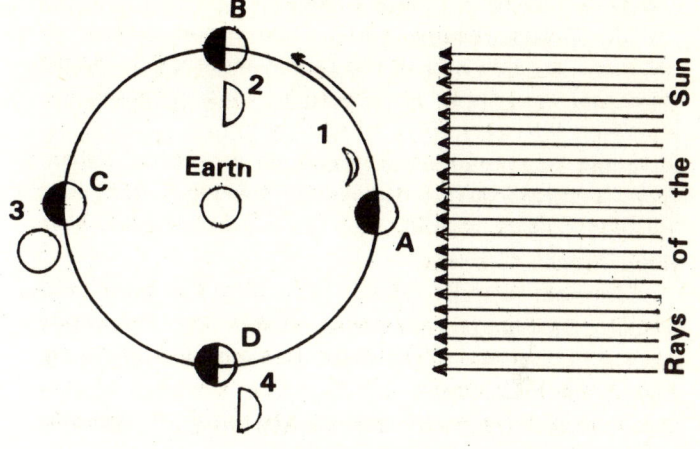

Fig. 4

It may be helpful briefly to illustrate here the cause of the moon's phases. Just as the earth revolves round the sun in a year, so the moon, every twenty-eight days, makes a similar revolution round the earth. As the earth itself has moved in the meantime, there is nearly thirty days between "New Moons" (or the moon reaching the sun's position). The rays of the sun (coming from the right of the diagram) always illuminate the part of the moon which is facing the sun. Thus when the moon is at A, we on earth cannot see the illuminated part at all. We see the edge of it, as a slender crescent (1) just afterwards— the "New Moon." When the moon has completed a quarter of its circuit it reaches B, and it is then seen as at (2)—the "First Quarter." Just over a week later it reaches C and is seen as a fully illuminated disc (3)—the "Full Moon". Finally, the last quarter is seen at D as (4). Thus, a change, or quarter, of the moon forms the natural basis of the week of seven days.

time of the Full Moon to that of the New Moon via the Last Quarter.

The Influence of the Lunar Changes

The period during which the moon waxes, its increase, the first half of the Lunar month, is a *period favourable to growth or expansion either material or spiritual*. The period in which the moon wanes, its decrease, is a *period unfavourable to growth or expansion: it corresponds to indrawing, lessening decay*—on all planes. Both periods, said the old Astrologers, have their uses to mankind.

Thus any activity which calls for the maximum possible growth and expansion should be *commenced during the increase of the moon*: sowing and planting, travel, the undertaking of any new venture, animal conception, investment, and inauguration of personal relationships.

Similarly, activities of a negative kind—reaping crops, extermination of pests, either animal, vegetable or parasitic, surgical excision of morbid growths, etc.—should be undertaken *during the decrease of the moon*.

Various Concerns, Occasions, Undertakings, Activities and Interests Which Fall Under the Rule of Each Planet

MERCURY: Travel, transport and communication of every kind: writing, television, radio, figuring, advertising, journalism, public speaking, education, and, all things that concern the young.

VENUS: Love, courtship, mating, marriage, art, music, decoration, dress, entertaining, holidays, dancing, gambling, peacemaking, pleasure of every kind, healing, social occasions of every kind, almsgiving.

MARS: Sports, games, hunting, fighting, wrestling, all that requires force, and strong and prompt action:

mechanical work, "stunting," surgery, public agitations and movements.

JUPITER: Business and trading of every kind, investments, banking and dealing with Bank officials; religious ceremonies and functions, seeking favours, settlements in litigation, ceremonial and philanthropic occasions of every kind where it is desired to help others and incidentally help one's self.

SATURN: Deep study, concentration, exact and just reasoning, mining, dealing in property and real estate, farming and gardening, drawing, mathematics, occasions requiring an absolutely balanced and unemotional state of mind.

URANUS: Everything "advanced," inventions, research, occultism, astrology, telepathy, idealistic movements, photography, wireless, aviation, electrical study and research. Intense and concentrated effort which is chiefly mental.

NEPTUNE: Sea travel, bathing, sensuous pleasures, inspiration, spiritual experiences, premonitions, spiritualistic "sittings," higher forms of music and art, divination of every kind.

i) Basic Traits of Character of People Born in January

The Zodiacal Sign of Capricorn commences on December 21st,[2] but for seven days, being overlapped by the "cusp" of the previous sign, it does not come into its full power until on or about December 28th. Hence, it is in full strength until January 20th,

---

[2] I here speak in a symbolic and cabbalistic sense, making use of Astrological terms in order to make my meaning clear to the reader. This remark applies to all other months which are included in my psychological survey of the twelve signs of the Zodiac.

and is then for seven days gradually losing its strength on account of becoming overlapped by the "cusp" of the incoming sign—Aquarius.

Persons born between January 20th and the 27th partake of the characteristics of both Capricorn and Aquarius and the same rule applies to all persons born within the "cusp" of any sign.

People born in this period have strong mental force, but they are, as a rule, generally misunderstood by others.

They are thinkers, reasoners, and make natural heads of business organisations or any form of government work.

They are independent and high-minded in all their actions, and detest being under the restraint of others.

They must be leaders in whatever they are engaged, or else they are inclined to lose their interest in their work.

They have strange ideas of love, duty, and social position, and for this reason they are often considered "odd," and do not fit in easily with their neighbours.

Even when not religious they have a deep devotional nature, and make great efforts to do good to others, but generally to masses of people rather than to individuals.

They often make excellent speakers, but not so much through oratory as by plain speaking; often too much so for their own good.

They generally make their greatest mistake by espousing the unpopular cause, the "under dog" in the fight, and so often make the bitterest enemies by their actions being misunderstood.

Such people generally feel their responsibilities too keenly, and often worry themselves into bad health.

They are quick in their intuitions of people and

things, but they are, as a rule, too easily discouraged, and lack self-confidence.

Although they appear cold, they have warm hearts towards suffering, and as a rule they give largely to charities, but subscribe more generously when giving to institutions than when giving to individuals.

If inclined to be religious they usually go to extremes, and become fanatical in their zeal.

They worship intellectual, clever people, and are deep thinkers; they rarely interfere with the affairs of others, but they will never stand interference from others.

They should aim for some form of public life, and in such careers they generally do best, such as in the government and in responsible positions of control and management of others.

They are inclined to excite bitter opposition but bear up against it with a philosophic spirit. Their home and family life is very often a troubled one. They feel "lonely-hearted" and misunderstood.

Friends: They usually make the most solid and best friendships with people who are born in their own period, viz. between December 21st to end of January, from April 20 to the end of May, and with their "central affinities," June 21 to July 20-27, and August 21 to September 20-27 (see Fig. 32).

Health: As a rule these people are more inclined to suffer from indigestion, rheumatism and pains in the feet.

Colours: The colours which give the most suitable vibrations to persons born in this period, and which are the most beneficial to them, are all tones of grey, all ranges of violet and purple, and also black.

Stones: The birth stones for this period are moonstones, pearls, and amethysts.

Some Famous Persons Born in this Part of the Year

The Earl of Beaconsfield	Dec.	21st
Josef Stalin	,,	21st
Marlene Dietrich	,,	27th
Woodrow Wilson	,,	28th
W.E. Gladstone	,,	29th
Rudyard Kipling	,,	30th
Prince Charlie (The Young Pretender)	,,	31st
Clement Attlee	Jan.	3rd
Herbert Morrison	,,	3rd
Joan of Arc	,,	6th
Sir Lawrence Alma Tadema	,,	8th
Wilkie Collins	,,	8th
Lord Curzon of Kedleston	,,	11th
Herman Goering	,,	12th
Gamal Nasser	,,	15th
Admiral, Earl Beatty	,,	16th
Benjamin Franklin	,,	17th
Compton Mackenzie	,,	17th
David Lloyd George	,,	17th
Cassius Clay	,,	18th
Lord Byron	,,	22nd
Francis Bacon	,,	22nd
Frederick the Great of Prussia	,,	24th
Wilhelm Furtwangler	,,	25th
W. Somerset Maugham	,,	25th
General MacArthur	,,	26th

ii) Basic Traits of Character of People Born in February

The Zodiacal Sign of Aquarius commences on January 21st, but for seven days, being overlapped by the "cusp" of the previous sign, it does not come into full power until on or about January 28th. From this date onward it is in full strength until February 19th. It is then for seven days gradually losing its strength on account of becoming overlapped by the "cusp" of the incoming sign—Pisces.

Those born in the "cusp" take from the qualities of both signs.

These natures generally feel very lonely in life; they are over-sensitive, and easily wounded in their feelings.

They read character instinctively, and for this reason they "see through" people too easily to be really happy.

They are not demonstrative in affection, but feel very deeply. If they "like" they fight to the bitter end for their friend; but if they dislike they are just as intense, and if they belong to the lower plane of humanity they will stick at nothing to avenge an injury or what they feel to be an injustice.

They are usually high-strung, and their nerves are generally overwrought; they often lose control of themselves and then they say or do things that they bitterly regret later.

They are generally very active for the public good, and will often give all they have to relieve the distress of others.

They are good reasoners, and are very successful in debate and argument, and difficult to convince. They generally have a scientific turn of mind.

They are excellent in business and finance when they apply their minds to such things, but as a general rule they are more successful for others, and make more money for others than for themselves.

If people born in this sign overcame their sensitiveness and developed their will-power, there is no position in life they could not attain. They generally succeed best in some large sphere of action, where they can feel their responsibilities for others. Those who are "awakened" in this sign usually leave a great name behind. They have "vision," imagination and invention.

They take a great interest in public meetings, gatherings of people, and public ceremonies. They love theatres and concerts, and like to be where crowds of people congregate, and yet they always have the feeling that *they are alone in life.*

They are very contradictory in the qualities they show under the call of circumstances; although themselves very high-strung and easily overwrought, *they have the very greatest power over excitable people and over the insane, and are in the run of their lives often brought much in contact with such classes.*

They have a quiet, controlling power with their eyes, and so subdue others.

Their greatest fault is that it generally takes some sudden call of circumstances to make them "make the most of themselves."

If born with money, these people rarely show what is in them. They are inclined in ordinary conditions to let their opportunities slip, or realise them only when it is too late. If, however, people born in this period belong to the lower order of humanity they lose all sense of honour and principle, and are extremely unreliable, tricky in money matters, dishonest, and unscrupulous in gaining what they desire.

Friends: In real friendship or love they get on best with those born from May 21 to June 20, and by adding the seven days of "the cusp" to about the end of the month. September 21 to October 20 or 27, and, as a rule, to November 20-27, or with those born in the centre of their triangle, as will be shown in Chapter 27, dealing with "Life's Triangles."

Health: These people are inclined to suffer most from the stomach, often through the nerves of the stomach in some peculiar manner that is difficult to relieve with ordinary medicine. Bad circulation often troubles them and there is often some delicacy of the eyes.

Colours: The most favourable colours for them are all shades of what are known as "electric shades," as electric blues and electric greys. These are the foundation colours for this period; for the exact colours for people born on each individual day see Chapter 28 on colours.

Stones: The birth stones for the period are sapphires, pink topazes, and moonstones.

Some Famous Persons Born in This Part of the Year

General Gordon	Jan	28th
Franklin D. Roosevelt	,,	30th
Charles Lindbergh	Feb.	4th
Sir Hartley Shawcross	,,	4th
Sir Henry Irving	,,	6th
Charles Dickens	,,	7th
Lord Carson	,,	9th
Edison	,,	11th
Abraham Lincoln	,,	12th
Darwin	,,	12th
G.M. Trevelyan	,,	16th
Elizabeth Taylor	,,	17th
Arthur Bryant	,,	18th
Copernicus	,,	19th
David Garrick	,,	20th
Lord Baden-Powell	,,	22th
George Washington	,,	22nd

Samuel Pepys	,,	23rd
Handel	,,	23rd

iii) Basic Traits of Character of People Born in March

The Zodiacal Sign of Pisces commences on February 20th, but for seven days, being overlapped by the "cusp" of the previous sign, it does not come into its full power until about February 27th. From this date onwards it is in full strength until March 20th, and it is then for seven days gradually losing its strength on account of becoming overlapped by the "cusp" of the incoming sign—Aries.

These people possess a curiously natural understanding, which they do not obtain from books or study. They easily acquire, or rather absorb, knowledge, especially of the history of countries, travel, research, and like subject.

Although by nature generous, yet they are usually over-anxious about money matters, and inclined to worry about what their future position in life may be. This state of mind is, I think, largely due to *their dislike and dread of being dependent on others more than from any love of money*.

This quality makes them, however, much misunderstood, and they are often considered close in money matters when in reality they are not.

People born in this period often go back on their promises, especially on questions of money. They promise to give, on the impulse of the moment, but if they have time for reflection then the fear of future poverty forces them, as a rule, to break their promise or give perhaps, only one half of what they had stipulated.

These people are also more *mentally* ambitious than

otherwise. They may know their subject well in their mind, but they will hesitate and undervalue their own individuality if they find they have to put it to a test in any public manner.

They are inclined to brood and become melancholy, or to imagine all the world is against them and that they are being made martyrs of.

They have great fidelity and loyalty if trust is imposed on them, and great persistence in carrying out whatever work they have in their hands to perform, and they are generally found in positions of trust and responsibility for others.

Many artists, musicians and literary people are born in this period, but they must receive great encouragement ever to make the best of themselves.

They have great loyalty to friends or to any cause they take up, provided they feel they are trusted or looked up to. They are generally successful in all positions of responsibility, but at the same time they are not inclined to push themselves forward, and usually "wait to be asked" before giving their opinions.

They are great respecters of law and order, and uphold the conventions of whatever the social order in which they may be found.

The strongest and weakest characters are found in this sign. Some are inclined to gratify their innate sense of luxury and self-indulgence and, if this side of the nature is the one that controls, they are likely to be too easy-going, to be too receptive to their surroundings, to become influenced by false friends, to give way to fraudulent schemes and in some cases are inclined to become addicted to drugs or drink.

If, however, persons born in this part of the year find some purpose worth living for, they rise to the emergency as no others can. These are the people that one meets sometimes in life who surprise their friends by their sudden change of character.

All persons born in this part of the year have a dual element as the mainspring of their nature. It simply depends on which of the two roads they have decided to follow.

Persons born in this sign are highly emotional. If they belong to the *weak* side of it, they are easily influenced by the people with whom they are thrown into contact, but if they belong to the stronger side, their emotional nature can lift them up to any height.

They are generally fond of the sea and large expanses of water. If circumstances do not permit them to travel, they will, if they possibly can, make their homes where they can see the ocean, or on the side of some lake, or river.

In business they are good in dealing with shipping and trade with foreign countries.

Sea captains, sailors of all kinds, also travellers, are often found under this sign.

Almost all have a curiously mystical side to their nature as well as the practical. They are often classed as superstitious, the occult in all its forms appealing to them in one way or another.

They love to search out or investigate the unknown, the philosophical, or the mysterious. Although generous, they do not allow their generous instincts to get the better of them, unless they are under the influence of someone they love. In such a case they become easily influenced and are as likely as not to give away all they possess.

If people born in this sign overcame their sensitiveness and developed their will-power, there is no position in life they could not attain.

Friends : They find their most lasting friendships

with people born in their own period or between June 21 and July 20, and on account of "the cusp" to about the end of the month (see Fig. 30); and with their "central affinities," August 21 to September 20-27, also October 21 to November 20-27 (see Fig. 30).

Health : As regards health, people born in this period are mostly inclined to suffer from nerves, insomnia, despondency, and poor circulation, anaemia. They often have intestinal trouble. They should, if possible, live in bright, sunny, dry climates, and take a great amount of fresh air and exercise. They are fond of travel, are restless, and love to be continually on the move.

Colours : The colours most suitable to them are all shades of mauve, violet, and purple. These are the foundation colours of this period; for the exact colours for people born on each individual day see Chapter 28 on colours.

Stones : The birth stones for this period are agates, sapphires, amethysts, and emeralds.

Some Famous Persons Born in
This Part of the Year

Joseph Jefferson	Feb.	20th
Cardinal Newman	,,	21st
James Russell Lowell	,,	22nd
Chopin	,,	22nd
W. Dean Howells	Mar.	1st
George Pullman	,,	3rd
Michaelangelo	,,	6th
Elizabeth Barrett Browning	,,	6th
M. Molotov	,,	9th
Harold Wilson	,,	11th
Albert Einstein	,,	14th
The Prince Imperial (Napoleon)	,,	16th

Rudolf Nureyev	,,	17th
Robert Donat	,,	18th
David Livingstone	,,	19th
Ibsen	,,	20th
William Lecky	,,	20th

iv) Basic Traits of Character of People Born in April

The Zodiacal Sign of Aries commences on March 21st, but for seven days, being overlapped by the "cusp" of the previous sign, it does not come into its full power until about March 27th. From this date onwards, it is in full strength until April 19th. It is then for seven days gradually losing its strength on account of becoming overlapped by the "cusp" of the incoming sign—Taurus.

People born in this section of the year have usually strong will power and great obstinacy of purpose.

They are born fighters in every sense of the word; they have also the greatest ability as organisers on a large scale, such as in the organisation of big schemes or as the heads of big businesses, and also in the organisation of armies or development of countries.

They seem naturally to resent all criticism, and the only way to offset this in them is by quiet logic, reason, and proof.

These people are intensely independent in work. They must do everything in their own way, and if they are interfered with by others they generally make a muddle of their plans or step back and let the other person take their place.

As a rule they are unhappy in their domestic life, for they rarely meet members of the opposite sex who understand them, and if opposition does not upset them from this point it usually does through their children.

Yet these people, be they men or women, crave for affection and sympathy more than anything else, and this is generally the rock on which they are finally wrecked if they have not the good fortune to meet their right affinities.

As far as material success or power is concerned, there are no heights to which persons born in this sign cannot climb—provided they "keep their heads." Success, however, is often their undoing, praise and flattery are inclined to make them have "swelled heads".

They are inclined to lack caution, being by nature impulsive and quick in thought and action.

They go to extremes in all things, are frank and outspoken, and inclined to make enemies by want of tact. They are enormously ambitious ; as a rule they succeed in life and amass money and position.

The lower type of this sign will stick at nothing to accomplish their purpose. The higher type are good masters, but at the same time severe in discipline and more or less exacting in the service they expect from others.

Both classes have a distinct desire to peer into the future, perhaps because they are impatient for things to develop. They are inclined to prophesy what will take place, and are often very gifted in this direction.

As a general rule, the men born in this part of the year suffer a great deal through their affections ; they seldom understand women, and make great mistakes in their relations with them.

For both sexes, their greatest happiness comes from work and the overcoming of obstacles.

Persons born in this sign seldom get through life without receiving cuts, wounds, or blows to the head, either from accidents or violence.

Friends : They will find their more lasting friend-hips and affections with those born in their own period or between July 21 and August 20-27, and from November 21 to December 20-27; and also from the centre of their triangle, September 21 to October 20-27, as I have explained in my chapter on "Life's Affinities (Fig. 29).

Health : People born in this period should try to obtain more sleep than almost any other class. They overwork their brains, and are inclined to suffer from all things that concern the head,—from headache, trouble with the eyes. They are also likely to have eruptions on the face and head. And they are liable to get cuts and wounds in the head, and they usually run danger from fire. They seldom get through life without a good deal of medical attention.

Colours : The most harmonious colour for them is all shades of red,—crimson, rose, and pink,—but when ill all shades of blue and violet are most soothing and beneficial to them. For the exact colours for people born on each individual day, see Chapter 28 on colours.

Stones : The birth stones for this period are rubies, garnets, and bloodstones.

Some Famous Persons Born in This Part of the Year

Arturo Tuscanini	Mar.	25th
Robert Bunsen	,,	31st
Bismarck	April	1st
Charlemagne	,,	2nd
Lord Lister	,,	5th
David Frost	,,	7th
Albert, King of the Belgians	,,	8th
John Gielgud	,,	14th
Sir John Franklin	,.	16th

Adolf Hitler	,,	20th
Bishop Heber	,,	21st
Yehudi Menuhin	,,	22nd
James Anthony Froude	,,	23rd
Shakespeare	,,	23rd
Oliver Cromwell	,,	24th
Sir Stafford Cripps	,,	24th

Basic Traits of Character of People Born in May

The Zodiacal Sign of Taurus commences on April 20th, but for seven days, being overlapped by the "cusp" of the previous sign, it does not come into its full power until on or about April 27th. From this date onwards it is in full strength until May 20th, and is then for seven days gradually losing its strength on account of becoming overlapped by the "cusp" of the incoming sign—Gemini.

People born in this section of the year have a curious power of dominating others, *even when not conscious of trying to do so.*

They are very unyielding in their determination, and are often called "stiff-necked" and obstinate, but when they love they are the most yielding and pliable of all, but only to those to whom they are attracted.

They have great power of endurance, both physical and mental, and can pass through enormous strains of fatigue as long as the excitement or determination lasts.

They have great ability to commit to memory from books, and are often very successful in literary work, but as a rule they love pleasure and society too much to make the best use of their gifts.

They make wonderful hosts and hostesses, and have great taste about food, and in the management of their houses they can make much out of little.

They make excellent directors, have good business intuition, but are generally considered richer than they really are, as they always dress well and look well.

They are governed by their sensations and by their loving nature, *but affection has a greater hold on them than passion.*

If they love, they are generous to the last degree, and will consider no sacrifice too great for the person they care for; if they are enemies, they will fight with the most determined obstinacy. But they always fight in the open, for they hate trickiness, double-dealing, or deceit.

They are easily influenced by their surroundings, and become morbid and morose when trying to live under uncongenial conditions.

Neither men nor women born in this period *should marry early; their first marriage is usually a mistake.*

They should always decide all important questions when they are alone, for they seem to be so much in touch with the minds of those around them that they get confused, and often imagine other people's thoughts and ideas are their own. They are also too easily misled by their emotions, sensations, or affections.

As a rule both sexes are jealous in their disposition, and their jealousy often drives them into acts of violence or sudden exhibition of temper, which they bitterly regret when the storm is over.

They forgive at the slightest show of feeling or kindness, and this side of their nature makes them do all kinds of things that the world calls stupid.

As leaders in any cause they inspire love and devotion, and often have great responsibility forced upon them.

They have an innate sense of harmony, rhythm and colour, and often succeed well in music, poetry and art.

Those born in this sign make the most faithful, loyal friends; also excellent public servants, officials, or as heads in Government positions or in the Army. They also make good, patient nurses and healers, and almost all have a keen love of gardening and flowers.

Health: In health, although, as a rule, endowed with a splendid constitution, they suffer with all things that affect the throat, nasal cavities and upper part of the lungs.

Friends: They will find their most lasting friendships with people born between August 21-27, and September 20-27, December 21 and January 20-27, and with their "central affinities" October 21 to November 20-27 (Fig. 32).

Colours: The colours most favourable to them are all shades of blue. Red is an exciting colour for them, and they should use it as little as possible. For the exact colours for people born on each individual day see Chapter 28 on colours.

Stones: The birth stones for this period are emeralds, turquoises, and lapis lazuli.

Some Famous Persons Born in this Part of the Year

Sir Thomas Beecham	April 29th
Haydn	" 31st
The Duke of Wellington	May 1st
Bing Crosby	" 2nd
Thomas Huxley	" 4th
Lord Rosebery	" 7th
Robert Browning	" 7th
Harry S. Truman	" 8th
Sir James Barrie	" 9th

Sir Arthur Sullivan	,,	12th
Alphonse Daudet	,,	13th
Margot Fonteyn	,,	18th
Sir Laurence Olivier	,,	22nd
Thomas Hood	,,	23rd
Queen Victoria	,,	24th
Duke of Marlborough	,,	24th

vi) Basic Traits of Character of People Born in June

The Zodiacal Sign of Gemini—The Twins—commences on May 21st, but for seven days, being overlapped by the "cusp" of the previous sign, it does not come into its full power until on or about May 28th.

From this date onwards it is in full strength until June 20th, and is then for seven days gradually losing strength on account of becoming overlapped by the "cusp" of the incoming sign—Cancer.

People born in this part of the year, namely, from May 21st to June 20th, and in the "cusp" to June 27th, have the characteristics of Gemini—The Twins—and are dual in character and in mentality.

The twin sides of their nature are perpetually pulling in opposite directions.

Their brains are subtle and brilliant, but they usually lack continuity of purpose.

Of all people they are the most difficult to understand; in temperament they are hot and cold almost at the same moment. They love with one side of their nature, and they are often critical or dislike with the other.

They are mentally very quick and keen, and in all matters where a subtle mentality is needed they can outdistance all rivals.

They are excellent in diplomacy, and dazzle their listeners by their wit and brilliancy, but they usually leave them no wiser than they were at the start.

They seldom, themselves, know what they want to achieve. At heart they are ambitious for social position; but when obtained they have already tired of it, and are ready to go in for something else or for something totally opposite.

If taken as they are, in their own moods, they are the most delightful people imaginable, but one must not attempt to hold them or to expect them to be constant to their ideas or plans.

They believe they are truthful, constant, faithful, and so they may be at the moment, but every moment to them has a separate existence.

They are always employed doing something, but they are restless, and as a rule want the thing they have not got.

They see quickly the weak points in those they meet, and can reduce all to nothing by wit, sarcasm, or mimicry.

They make clever actors, lawyers, lecturers, and a certain class of public speakers, all those who play a changing role in life's drama; but if endowed with unusually strong will power, and if they can *force themselves to stick to one thing, then they generally make brilliant successes of whatever they undertake in any sphere of life.*

They often succeed the best, as far as money is concerned, on the Stock Exchange or as Company Promoters or in the invention of new ways to get wealth in business, but their more suitable career is generally that which requires diplomacy, tact, and finesse.

In all matters of affection they are human puzzles.

They can love passionately and yet be inconstant at the same moment, and it is only their shield of diplomacy and exquisite tact that keeps them from often making a mess of their lives.

They are more generous to individuals than to institutions, for they act on impulse in giving as in everything else they do.

In appearance these people generally have a rather long, narrow head and face; good, keen, sharp-looking eyes. The hands, as a rule, are long, thin or bony; restless or always doing something. In nature they are inclined to have too many "irons in the fire" at the same moment.

The higher types are clever, capable, witty, subtle, with an odd sense of humour quite their own. As a rule they are very intellectual with a keen mentality that shows itself in anything they seriously take up. Worry, annoyance or undue mental strain breaks them down very rapidly, producing nervous prostration, brain exhaustion, and in some cases insanity.

The lower types are unscrupulous in finance and untruthful. They often make successful gamblers and company promoters of "get-rich-quick" schemes.

Either type make hosts of friends and are kind-hearted and generous to the person who fills their thoughts at the moment, but "out of sight, out of mind" explains their fits of "forgetfulness" as nothing else can.

Friends: Both types make their most lasting friendships with people born either in their own period of the year or from September 21 to October 20-27, January 21 to February 18-27, or with people born in the centre of their own triangle, from November 21 to December 20-27 (Fig. 31).

Health: They are more inclined to suffer from what

concerns the nervous system than anything else, both men and women are likely to have delicacy with the digestive organs. They are rather inclined to have chest trouble.

Colours: Their colours are silver, glistening white, and all shimmering things. For the exact colours for persons born on each day, see Chapter 28 on colours.

Stones: The birth stones for this period are white and red cornelians, sapphires, diamonds and all glittering jewels.

Some Fomous Persons Born in this Part of the Year

John F. Kennedy	May 29th
Charles II	" 29th
Bob Hope	" 29th
Sir Edward Elgar	June 2nd
Thomas Hardy	" 2nd
Richard Cobden	" 3rd
George V	" 3rd
Jefferson Davis	" 3rd
George III	" 4th
Sir Anthony Eden	" 12th
Ralph Waldo Emerson	" 15th
Gounod	" 17th
Earl Haig	" 19th
Julian Hawthorne	" 22nd
Sir Rider Haggard	" 22nd
Lord Louis Mountbatten	" 25th

vii) Basic Traits of Character of People Born in July

The Zodiacal Sign of Cancer commences on June 21st, but for seven days, being overlapped by the previous sign, it does not come into full power until on or about June 28th. From this date onwards it is in full strength until July 20th, and is then for seven days gradually losing its strength on account of becoming overlapped by the "cusp" of the incoming sign—Leo.

The Sign of Cancer, or the Crab, was so called by the ancients because the sun at this time of the year appears to advance and retreat in the heavens like the actions of a crab.

People born in this section of the year are full of contradictions, they have deep home interests, but are at the same time restless, and have a decided longing for travel and change, they are always making homes, rarely keeping them, and usually have more than the usual trouble in the homes they do succeed in making and in their domestic life.

They are generally over-anxious in financial matters, and make great efforts to gather in money; as a rule, they have unusual ups and downs in their early life, and it takes all their hard work to keep ahead, but once they get on their feet they generally keep there.

They are inclined to speculate, so as to make money quickly, but in all gambles they generally lose, whereas in business *they are as a rule most successful.*

They are industrious and hardworking in all they undertake, but from the standpoint of chance or luck they are seldom fortunate, but the most extraordinary and unexpected changes, for good or evil, seem always ready to come into their lives.

They are generally gifted with strong imaginations, and often make excellent artists, writers, composers, or musicians. At heart they are romantic and of a very loving and affectionate disposition.

They have a great dislike of being dictated to, but are most devoted and faithful when treated with confidence.

They have, however, most sensitive natures—perhaps more so than any other class of people—and if not understood they quickly give up or get depressed and melancholy. Above all, they require encouragement and appreciation.

They often make excellent psychics, and usually have a yearning after the mysterious.

They should never marry young, *for their nature seems to change at different stages of life.*

Like the symbol of "the Crab," which this part of the Zodiac represents, they advance and retreat both in work and ideas; they may reach a certain point in some definite plan or career, and then surprise everyone by stopping, or turning back at the most critical point.

People born in this part of the year often reach very high exalted positions. In their home lives, however, they usually go through a great deal of trouble, and are seldom surrounded by great happiness, no matter how successful they may appear in the eyes of the world.

Although of a deeply affectionate disposition they are seldom demonstrative, and are wrongly considered cold and unemotional.

Generally, they have splendid memories and store up knowledge of all kinds in their minds.

They have deep love for what they call "their own people," for family customs and for tradition.

Health: They are chiefly inclined towards gastric troubles, and they should be extremely careful in regard to shellfish and such things. Inflammatory diseases, such as rheumatism, are also likely to attack them, and trouble with the legs and feet.

Friends: Their affections or friendships last longest

with those who are born in their own period, June 21 to July 20-27, or from October 21 to November 20-27, or from February 19 to March 20-27, and also those who are in the centre of their triangle, December 21 to January 20-27, which I have explained in a subsequent chapter on "Life's Triangles." (Chapter 27).

Colours: The colours most in harmony for them are all shades of green, and cream and white. For the exact colours for persons born on each day see Chapter 28 on colours.

Stones: The birth stones most favourable for this period are pearls, diamonds, opals, crystals, cats's-eyes, and moonstones.

Some Famous Persons Born in This Part of the Year

James I of England	June 28th
Charles Laughton	July 1st
Gluck	" 2nd
Nathaniel Hawthorne	" 4th
Gertrude Lawrence	" 4th
Cecil Rhodes	" 6th
Edward Heath	" 9th
John Calvin	" 10th
John Quincy Adams	" 11th
Sir Joshua Reynolds	" 16th
Lord Balfour	" 25th
George Bernard Shaw	" 26th
Mussolini	" 29th

viii) Basic Traits of Character of People Born in August

The Zodiacal Sign of Leo commences on July 21st, but for seven days, being overlapped by the "cusp" of the previous sign, it does not come into its full power until on or about July 28th. From this date onwards it is in full strength until August 20th and is then for seven days gradually losing its strength on account of becoming overlapped by the "cusp" of the incoming sign—Virgo.

People born in this period always aim to get above the common herd of humanity, and they themselves in turn are naturally attracted to strong personalities—in fact, they will forgive any fault in the people they like so long as they have individuality and purpose.

These people represent what might be termed the heartforce of humanity. They are overflowing with sympathy, and are generally generous to a fault.

They will defend a friend in the face of a million foes and disloyalty and deceit are the only things that can break their great hearts.

They are themselves exceptionally truthful and honest, but they often get terribly deceived, and have a tendency in the end to become bitter, severe, and over-critical.

They are usually lucky in money matters, often having money given to them from unthought-of sources: but they crave love above all, and this is the one thing they seldom get.

They have the power to inspire others, and as leaders—like Napoleon, born in this Sign—they can lead their men through fire or death. They are intensely proud, and often are easily wounded at this point in their nature.

They have an extremely independent spirit; they detest control or being dictated to. They have great tenacity of purpose and will power and if once they put their mind on some plan, purpose or position, they usually reach their goal in spite of every difficulty or obstacle.

Such persons must, however, be always actively

employed. If forced by circumstances out of the heat and stress of life, they often become morbid and despondent.

As a rule they are extremely patient and long-suffering, but if once roused, they know no fear and do not even know when they meet defeat, or acknowledge it when they do.

They make enemies by their frankness of speech and their hatred of anything underhand or that savours of subterfuge.

They have great tenacity of purpose, determination, and will power if they once put their mind on some purpose, but they usually attempt the most daring and difficult things.

Great soldiers, leaders in finance, and public men are often born in this period.

As a rule, people born in this period feel isolated and lonely in life, and if not actively employed in some work or purpose they become melancholy and despondent.

Friends They would find their most lasting friendships with people born in their own period or from March 21 to April 19-27, with their "central affinities" January 21 to February 18-28 (Fig. 29), and November 21 to December 20-27; and, strange to say, all those people born on the 1st, 10th, 19th, or 28th of any month, for the reason that these numbers accord and have a sympathetic attraction to the Number of the Sun, *which is the number of this period*. These numbers and dates are fully explained elsewhere in this book.

Health: These people are inclined to suffer from the heart, palpitations, pains in the head and ears.

Colours: Their most suitable colours are all shades of yellow, orange, pale green, and white. For the exact colours for persons born on each day see Chapter 28 on colours.

Stones: The birth stones for this period are topazes, amber, and rubies.

Some Famous Persons Born in
This Part of the Year

Alexandre Dumas	July 28th
Henry Moore	" 30th
King Haakon VII. of Norway	Aug. 3rd
Sir Harry Lauder	" 4th
Neil Armstrong	" 5th
Alexander Fleming	" 6th
Field-Marshal Sir William Slim	" 6th
Dean Farrar	" 7th
President Hoover	" 10th
George IV of England	" 12th
Napoleon I	" 15th
Louis XVI	" 23rd
Bert Harte	" 25th
Prince Albert, Consort of Queen Victoria	" 26th
George Hegel	" 27th

ix) Traits of Character of People Born in September

The Zodiacal Sign of Virgo commences on August 21st, but for seven days, being overlapped by the "cusp" of the previous sign, it does not come into its full power until on or about August 29th. From this date onwards it is in full strength until September 20th, and is then for seven days gradually losing its strength on account of becoming overlapped by the "cusp" of the incoming sign-Libra.

People born in this period are as a rule generally successful in life. They have keen, good intellects, are very discriminating about those with whom they associate, and in all business matters they have good judgment, and are not easily imposed upon or deceived.

They are usually materialistic in their views of life, and analyse and reason everything *from their own way of thinking outwards*.

They make good literary critics, being quick to see the weak points, and at the same time they are rapid readers and endowed with wonderful memories.

They are extremely fond of harmony in their surroundings, have excellent taste about their house and dress, and always want things in good taste, and elegant.

They are not so apt to be originators as they are to carry out some plan or work that appeals to them and with others have failed to finish, and in the execution of almost all things to which they put their minds they achieve success.

They are fastidious about their personal appearance, have a great respect for rank and position, and are great supporters of the law and the law's decisions.

They make excellent lawyers and debaters, but they tend towards supporting precedents more than originating any new law.

They succeed well in business, but more from their steady, industrious persistency than from evolving new ideas.

They are inclined to become wrapped up in themselves and their own ideas, and often become selfish in the close pursuit of their aims.

They are more capable of going to extremes in good and evil than any other type. If they develop a love for money they will stick at nothing to acquire it, and this type is often considered cunning and crafty at the expense of others.

They can adapt themselves to almost any pursuit in life.

In love they are the most difficult to understand, the very best and the very worst of men and women being born in this part of the year.

In their early years nearly all are intensely virtuous and pure-minded, as might be expected, being born in the Sign of Virgo—the Virgin.

If they change they do so with a vengeance and become the exact reverse, but, on account of their inborn respect of the law and their natural cleverness, they succeed in covering up their lapses better than any other class They have often a tendency to indulge in drugs or drink.

Health: In health, as a rule, they are less liable to diseases than persons born in any other part of the year, yet the strange thing about them is that they are always imagining themselves to have every illness that they may happen to read about.

They are very refined in their tastes as far as food is concerned, and must have things nicely put before them or they will lose their appetites.

They are extremely sensitive to their surroundings; the least inharmony or annoyance affects their nervous system and upsets their digestive organs.

They have a tendency to have chest trouble, and to suffer from neuritis in the shoulder and arms.

As this sign of the Zodiac appears to be intimately associated with the Solar Plexus, people born in this part of the year need sunlight and fresh air more than any other class of individual.

They should live as much as possible in the open air, and when run down or ill a few weeks in the country will work marvels with them.

As a rule, they retain their youth through life in the most wonderful manner.

If badly mated, or living under inharmonious marriage conditions, they easily fall into ill health or get extremely despondent.

They should never drink alcohol, as it seems to be more a poison to them than to any other class.

Friends: They will find their most lasting friendships with those born in their own Sign, also from April 20 to May 20-27, and with their "central affinities," February 19 to March 20-27 and December 21 to January 20-27 (Fig. 32).

Colours: Their most suitable colours are all very pale shades and silvery, shimmering materials. For the exact colours for persons born on each days see Chapter 28 on colours.

Stones: The birth stones for this period are emeralds, diamonds, and pearls.

Some Famous Persons Born in this Part of the Year

Goethe	Aug.	28th
Oliver Wendell Holmes	,,	28th
Queen Wilhelmina of Holland	,,	31st
Henry George	Sept.	2nd
Sir Charles Dilke	,,	4th
Sir Norman Birkett	,,	6th
Queen Elizabeth I	,,	7th
Lord Oxford and Asquith	,,	12th
Chateaubriand	,,	14th
President Taft	,,	15th
President Diaz	,,	15th
Bonar Law	,,	16th
Sir Edward Marshall Hall	,,	18th
Greta Garbo	,,	18th
Peter Sellers	,,	19th

Twiggy ,, 20th
Sophia Loren ,, 21st

x) Basic Traits of Character of People Born in October

The Zodiacal Sign of Libra commences on September 21st, but for seven days, being overlapped by the "cusp" of the previous sign, it does not come into full power until on or about September 28th. From this date onwards it is in full strength until October 20th, and is then for seven days gradually losing power on account of becoming overlapped by the incoming sign —Scorpio.

This sign of Libra is represented in symbolism as The Balance.

People born in this Sign are positive and decisive in their thoughts and actions. They have great foresight and intuition, and are generally seen at their best when acting on first impressions.

They are often very psychic, have curious presentiments, and would make very devout spiritualists, theosophists, and occultists, and yet so strongly endowed are they with the desire to reason out everything that their *love of exact proof* usually overwhelms their psychic powers.

They are often very successful as speculators, but they have little regard for the value of money, and have as a rule great ups and downs in their careers.

In symbolism they represent a "balance." They seem always trying mentally to balance things and get an even judgment.

Large numbers of them seem to drift naturally into the study of law, and in it they generally make a name as lawyers, barristers, or judges.

They are also often found in public life, but again it is with their innate desire to adjust the balance of things by making laws for the betterment of their fellows.

They have great reverence for knowledge, and often spend their lifetime in study and research in some particular subject, again weighing and balancing every side of the question in the most conscientious manner. For this reason they make excellent doctors, but generally make their name as masters of some particular line of study more than as general practitioners.

In all careers that require depth of study, thoughtfulness, and balance they succeed best, but all professional walks of life are as a rule well suited to them.

In marriage they are seldom happy. In affection they appear to weigh and balance matters too much.

They crave for the peace and happiness of home life, but in doing so they generally become too exacting, and the result is more often than not, disaster. They have the compensation, however, of making large circles of friends and acquaintances, and are largely sought after as companions.

Friends : They would find their most lasting friendships and unions with persons born between January 21 and February 18-27, May 21 and June 20-27, and with those bron in their own Sign or with their "central affinities," March 21 to April 19-26, as shown by Fig. 31.

Health : People born in this period are inclined to suffer most from nerves and depression of spirits, also from pains in the back and kidneys and severe headaches.

Colours : The most suitable colours for them are all shades of blue, violet, purple and mauve. For the exact colours for persons born on each day see Chapter 28 on colours.

Stones: The birth stones for this period are the opal and the pearl.

Some Famous Persons Born in this Part of the Year

Julius Caesar	Sept.	23rd
Brigitte Bardot	,,	28th
Lord Roberts	,,	30th
Marshal Foch	Oct.	2nd
Mahatma Gandhi	,,	2nd
Sir Alfred Munnings	,,	8th
Christiaan Barnard	,,	8th
George II. of England	,,	10th
Ralph Vaughan Williams	,,	12th
General Eisenhower	,,	14th
P.G. Wodehouse	,,	15th
Oscar Wilde	,,	16th
Frederick III. of Germany	,,	18th
President Adams	,,	19th
Samuel Taylor Coleridge	,,	21st
Martin Luther	,,	22nd
Faraday	,,	22nd
Sarah Berndardt	,,	22nd

xi) Basic Traits of Character of People Born in November

The Zodiacal Sign of Scorpio commences on October 21st, but for seven days, being overlapped by the "cusp" of the previous sign, it does not come into its full power until on or about October 28th. From this date onwards it is in full strength until November 20th and is then for seven days gradually losing its strength on account of becoming overlapped by the "cusp" of the incoming sign—Sagittarius.

The Sign of Scorpio is represented by two symbols, that of the Scorpion and the Eagle.

People born in this section of the year seem to be a mass of contradictions. The best and the worst seem to make this period their chosen battlefield.

Up to nearly twenty years of age they are usually extremely pure-minded, virtuous, and religious, but once their nature is roused they are often found to swing in the opposite direction. At the same time the greatest saints have been found in this period.

All remain, however, intensely, emotional, which is the very keynote of their character in all its phases.

They have great magnetic power, and as speakers appeal to the emotions and sentiments of their public more than to logic, but they sway their audiences as they choose.

They have excellent power in writing, are intensely dramatic in their gift of description, and are unusually versatile in their talents.

In dangers and in sudden crises they are cool and very determined, and many of the very best surgeons have been found in this period.

Their worst fault is that they are too adaptable to the people with whom they come in contact.

They are often great humanitarians, with great plans for making the world right, and praise will often force them to do great things in the world for their fellow-men.

They nearly always, however, lead double lives— one for the eyes of the world and another for themselves.

They have clever ideas in business and politics, but they are best advisers of others. They should be warned against "putting off things until tomorrow," for procastination is one of their besetting sins.

They are mental fighters, and are most subtle in arguments. They make good organisers and generals on paper, but detest bloodshed and strife in actual life.

For this reason they gain a reputation as peacemakers, and in fact, they usually excel in settling other people's quarrels and bringing enemies together to shake hands.

No class of people make more friends or have more enemies than those born in this period, but their strong personality carries them through like a resistless wave.

The sex quality is an enormous factor in their lives. The women attract men and the men attract women; but in cases where the will and ambition are dominant these people can keep the curb on their strong sex-natures.

People in this Sign should, above all, be encouraged to have ambition, *for it is the one thing that will save them; for it they will make any sacrifice or deny themselves any pleasure*, and so accomplish more work than any other class.

They are inclined to be selfish and to sacrifice everything to the need of the moment; but, in contradiction to this, if they succeed there are no people more generous in paying back tenfold for any help they may have received.

In their home life the men are inclined to be dogmatic, and expect to rule, but their influence over women is so great that they are almost always forgiven.

With their strong magnetic influence they possess generally a strange psychological power over others; they make natural healers, for they give or their great vitality to others, and when their emotions or sympathies are roused they love to give and to help, and will face any danger to be of assistance.

Sooner or later, they generally become interested in occult matters, they readily develop unusual clairvoyant powers, and quite often gain fame and distinction as writers, painters or poets. They are natural philosophers, deep students of Nature, and observe and analyse other persons' characters better than any other class.

They are generally loved and adored by those who know them, but there are very few born under this sign who at some stage in their career escape being attacked by calumny of scandal.

Persons born in this generally have, or make, two sources of income. As a rule they go through a great deal of trouble, difficulty and often privation in their early years; such trials seem to increase their will-power and ambition, and sooner or later success and fame nearly always crown their efforts.

Friends: They will find their most lasting friendships and unions with people born in their own period and between June 21 and July 20-27, from February 19 to March 20-27, and with the centre of their "Life's Triangle" (Fig. 30), namely, those born from April 20 to May 20-27.

Health: These people as a rule are very slight and thin in their early years, but put on weight and are inclined to corpulency after reaching middle life. Later the heart is inclined to be their weakest organ, and they should be careful not to overstrain it in exercise, or in work.

Colours: The colours most suitable for persons of this period are all shades of crimson and blue. For the exact colours for persons born on each day see Chapter 28 on colours.

Stones: The birth stones for this period are the turquoise, the ruby, and all red stones.

Some Famous Persons Born in This Part of the Year

Pablo Picasso	Oct.	25th
President Roosevelt	,,	27th
Captain Cook	,,	28th
Generalissimo Chiang Kai-Shek	,,	31th
"Cheiro"	Nov.	1st
Marie Antoinette of France	,,	2nd
President Harding	,,	2nd
Vivien Leigh	,,	5th
Billy Graham	,,	9th
Richard Burton	,,	7th
William Hogarth	,,	10th
Saint Augustine	,,	13th
Sir William Herschel	,,	15th
Field-Marshal Lord Montgomery	,,	17th
President Garfield	,,	19th
Charles I. of England	,,	19th
Thomas Chatterton	,,	20th
George Eliot	,,	22nd
Charles de Gaulle	,,	22nd
Grace Darling	,,	24th

xii) Basic Traits of Character of People Born in December

The Zodiacal Sign of Sagittarius commences on November 21st, but for seven days, being overlapped by the "cusp" of the previous sign, it does not come into its full power until on or about November 28th. From this date onwards it is in full power until December 20th, and is then for seven days gradually losing its strength on account of being overlapped by the incoming Sign—Capricorn.

This Sign of Sagittarius is symbolically represented either by the figure of an archer, or by a half-horse, half-man, the man part shooting an arrow from a bow.

Those born in this section of the year are executive, fearless and determined in all they undertake.

They are apt to be too decisive and too outspoken in their speech, and so are often misjudged in their criticism, and make bitter enemies.

They concentrate all their attention on whatever they are doing at the moment, *and seem to see no other way but theirs until their effort is made.*

They are, however, the great workers; they never seem to tire until they drop with fatigue.

They are generally very honourable, but chiefly when they feel others are placing implicit confidence in them. Brutally truthful, they resent deception, and unmask any attempt to deceive others even when such action is against their own interests. There are two distinct classes that exist in this period. The people of one section have their ideals of life extremely high and any appeal to do good is met with an immediate response.

Those of this first class are the salt of the earth in their care for their employees and people under them.

They have great enterprise in business, but never feel themselves confined to any one line; because they have been successful in some one thing is no reason whatever that they must follow it through life. For this reason one often finds the men of this period change from clergymen to stockbrokers, or from professors to followers of trade; while the women successful in one line of work will just as quickly throw themselves heart and soul into some entirely new study.

As a rule, perhaps from their intense concentration and will power, they are successful in whatever they do, and they should *always be allowed a free hand in choosing their vocation.*

The people of the second class born in this period are easily recognised; first, by their sharp criticism of every one else's efforts for good and by their petty meanness in all matters that concern money.

People of this second class are eaten up with selfish ambition. In any country in which they live they force their way into government positions. They crave titles and are snobs beyond description. They are also hypocrites and religious bigots of the worst class, the simplest student of humanity, after a little observation, will never confound them with those of the other class in the same Sign.

Nearly all classes in this Sign are devoted to music. They often make brilliant musicians.

They are, however, inclined to go to extremes in all things, and make sudden decisions, or change their minds rapidly, for which they may have regrets, *but they are too proud to acknowledge their error*.

The men of this Sign nearly always marry on impulse and regret it afterwards, but they are too proud to show their regrets and too conventional to appeal to the courts for assistance, so they often pass for models of the most married happiness even when they are wretched.

The women born in this Sign are, as a rule, the nobler of the two; they love to make their husbands successful and will sacrifice everything to that end. They are generally chaste and have an intense love of home, and even when unhappily married they make the best of a bad bargain.

They are great church-goers.

They venerate law and order and make the best of mothers.

People born in this period, even when successful,

should never cease to be actively employed—inactivity for them would mean despondency and an early decay.

Friends : Their most lasting unions and friendships would be made with people born from March 21 to April 19-26, and July 21 to August 20-27, or in their own period; and they will also find excellent companions in those born in the centre of their triangle—namely, from May 21 to June 20-27 (Fig. 29).

Health : They will be more inclined to suffer form rheumatism than from any other disease, also from a delicacy of the throat and lungs, and skin troubles. They also, especially in their latter years, suffer from the nervous system.

Colours : Their most suitable colours are all shades of violet and mauve and violet-purple. For the exact colours for persons born on each day see Chapter 28 on colours.

Stones : Their most favourable stones are amethysts and sapphires.

Some Famous Persons Born in this Part of the Year

Sir Winston Churchill	Nov. 30	Warren Hastings	Dec. 6
"Mark Twain"	,, 30	Joseph Conrad	,, 6
Queen Alexandra	Dec. 1	Sir Osbert Sitwell	,, 6
Thomas Carlyle	,, 4	John Osborne	,, 14
Maria Callas	,, 4	Noel Coward	,, 16
Sir Hamilton Harty	,, 5	Sir Humphry Davy	,, 17
Henry VI	,, 6	Prince George	,, 20
Admiral Lord Jellicoe	,, 6	Andrew Carnegie	,, 25
Sir Walter Scott	,, 6	Marlene Dietrich	,, 27

25

Occult Significance of Numbers with Birth Dates

AT FIRST SIGHT IT may seem extravagant to say that people may easily and quickly learn whether or not they will be in harmony with those they meet by applying the following few simple rules which I have found, by long experience, cover one of the mysterious sides of occultism in regard to Numbers.

Even a few tests will prove to those who care to try that there is a great deal in the curious theory which I am about to lay before the readers of this book.

When dealing with such subjects I endeavour to write in such a clear and simple way that even those who have had no experience whatever in occult studies may be able to understand and act on my remarks, and make experiments for themselves.

Only Nine Numbers

In the first place, it is necessary to grasp the idea that there are really only nine Numbers, that is to say, that the foundation numbers of all science and all calculation lie between the Number 1 and the Number 9, and that all others are only a repetition of these numbers, and nothing more. For example, a 10 is a 1 with the 0 added, and 11 is, when added together, a 2, a 12 is a 3, a 13 is a 4, and so on up to any number that one may examine.

The occult side of this may be found in the fact that man has been called into being by the Seven Creative Planets. Beyond these seven planets there are two others, namely Uranus and Neptune, whose domain is considered to rule the mental or spirit plane of things, and the numbers representing them have been from time immemorial incorporated with the numbers of the Sun and Moon (the only two planets that have been given double numbers as follows: Mars 9; Mercury, 5; Jupiter, 3; Venus, 6; Saturn, 8.

In this way the entire nine numbers on which life has built all its calculations are accounted for, and so are also all the planets of our solar system, form the earth itself up to the "fixed stars," behind which, the ancients said, the Creator of all creates.

Birth Dates

Taking the above explanation as a starting basis, the reader may now be able to follow my theory—a theory, by the way, that has taken me years to work out and prove, which is that *independent of what part of the year one may be born in, a curious sympathy and attraction will be found to exist between all those who have the same number for their birth date.* For example, a person born, say, on the 1st of any month will find others that are born on the 1st, 10th, 19th, or 28th, of any month more sympathetic than people not born on these dates.

An exception must, however, be made for all people born under the Sun's and Moon's numbers, which are, Sun, 1-4, and Moon, 2-7, as such people are always attracted and "natural friends" to one another; but all other numbers attract, as it were, their own class.

Affinities in Human Beings

Such attraction is, however, *more mental than*

physical. It is, as it were, that the planets of the same numbers rule the mind and make those born on the same dates have a similarity *and sympathy of thought to one another*.

Physical attraction takes place if the birth date of two people should be in certain months of the year (see chapter on "Life's Affinities"), and if in such a case the numbers should also be found to be in sympathy then we would have both mental and physical attraction, which would make a union of friendship unbreakable. This is an illustration of that often misused expression that "marriages are made in heaven."

Such marriages are, in fact, made in the heavens by the planets and places of the year creating affinities in human beings, which has been so eloquently expressed in the following well-known verse:

"Two shall be born the whole wide world apart
And speak in different tongues, and take no thought
Each of the other's being, and no heed.
And these o'er unknown seas to unknown lands
Shall cross, escaping wreck, defying death,
And all unconsciously shape every act,
And bend each wandering step unto this end
That one day out of darkness they shall meet
And read life's meaning in each other's eyes."

In the following chapter I shall deal with this curiously interesting subject, and also show the affinities of those born in certain months with others.

26

Life's Triangles and Affinities

AS I STATED in the previous chapter, independent of what part of the year one may be bore in, a sympathy and attraction will be found to exist between all those persons who have the same number for their birth date. For example, a person born, say, on the 1st of any month will find others born on the 1st, 10th, 19th or 28th of any part of the year sympathetic and attractive to him, because, as explained in the preceding chapter, all these numbers, by natural addition, have the number 1 for their root. A 10 is simply a 1 with a 0; a 19 is also a 1, for 1 added to 9 would make 10, which, as before explained, is a 1. And so on with any number whose parts must be added together to get what is called the "spirit of the number."

The next rule is that the double numbers of the Sun and Moon, which are Sun, 1-4, and Moon, 2-7, are sympathetic to one another, as they are also to their own series when taken as single numbers, such as a person born on the 2nd is sympathetic to those born on the 7th, 11th, 16th, 20th, 25th and 29th, which make, as explained earlier, all twos and sevens.

These persons would be sympathetic also to people born under what is called the Sun's numbers, 1-4, namely, 1st, and 4th, 10th, 13th, 19th, 22nd, and 31st, which, as explained, make ones and fours.

As I have also stated, these sympathies are increased

according to the month in which people happen to be born, and which I will now endeavour to explain clearly.

Life's Triangles

The twelve months of the year are divided by four triangles, which fit in together and present in the most perfect symbolism the four elements necessary to human life, and from which life draws its very existence,—namely, Fire, Water, Air, and Earth.

In order to fix these four triangles clearly in one's mind, I would advise my readers to first draw a triangle, and place at its three points the sections of the year as I will indicate them, which is also shown in the accompanying plates.

Triangle of Fire

Taking the triangle of Fire, place March 21 to April 19 at the top, July 21 to August 20 at the second point, on the left-hand side, and November 21 to December 20 on the third point, on the right base of the triangle. You will then have what are called the "Fire affinities", in their proper places.

If the lines of your triangle are of equal length, and if you draw a line from each apex to cut the centre of the line at its base, the months thus indicated, which would necessarily be a period equally distant in that part of the year from the two sections at each point, you would then get when I call "the central affinity" which as a rule is equally strong although totally *opposite in character*. (Fig. 29).

Now if you were to find that a person born in any of these four sections is also born on a sympathetic number, as earlier explained, you would then have *a mental and physical affinity attracted in every sense to one another*.

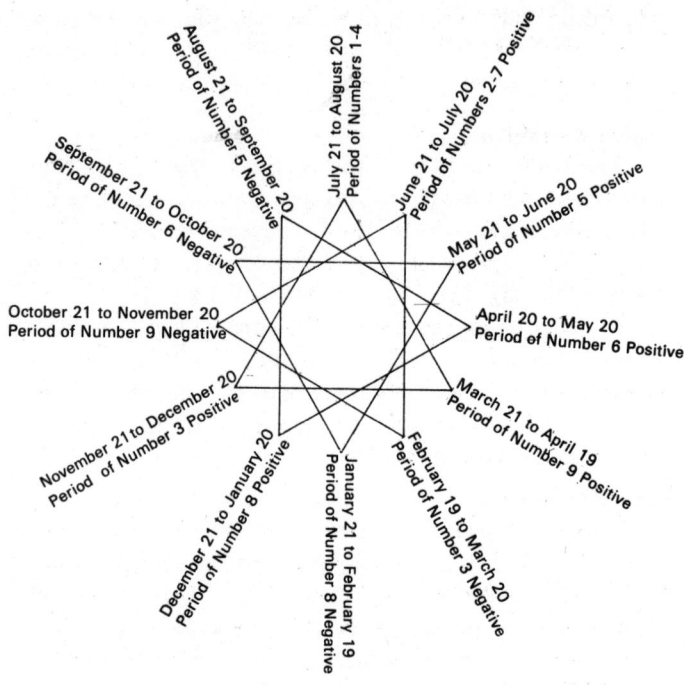

Fig. 5 : Life's Triangles

The Water Triangle

The symbolic triangle representing the element of water is formed in the following manner. Place the section June 21 to July 20 at the top, the section October 21 to November 20 at the left lower angle, and the section February 19 to March 20 at the lower right angle, and the Water triangle becomes complete. You again draw the apex lines from each point, as indicated in the illustration, and work out the sympathetic attraction of the numbers to one another. (Fig. 30).

The Air Triangle

The symbolic triangle of the element of Air is formed in the following manner: Draw a triangle as before. Place at the top the section May 21 to June 20; at the left-hand point place September 21 to October 20; at the right, January 21 to February 18. Draw lines from each apex as before described, and work out the sympathetic attraction of the numbers to one another.

Tha Earth Triangle

The symbolic triangle of the element of Earth is formed in the following manner: Draw a triangle as before. Place at the top the section April 20 to May 20 at the left-hand point place August 21 to September 20; at the right, December 21 to January 20. Draw lines from each apex as described, before and work out the sympathetic attraction of the numbers to one another.

When these four triangles are constructed the entire year is represented and people born in the sections symbolised by the different triangles will be attracted as affinities to one another, *especially if their numbers should also be found to harmonise.*

People born, however, in such triangles as are symbolised by Air and Water are favourable to one another, although one could not call them affinities. It is the same with the Air and Earth triangles, and with the Air and Fire, but in all such cases the Air people will dominate the others more by their mental than by their physical attraction.

The Earth and Water people can also blend, and make, as it were, solid material things together; but the mixture will be more that of the material than of the spiritual.

Fire and Earth people can also get on together, for in this symbolism the Fire will warm the Earth and

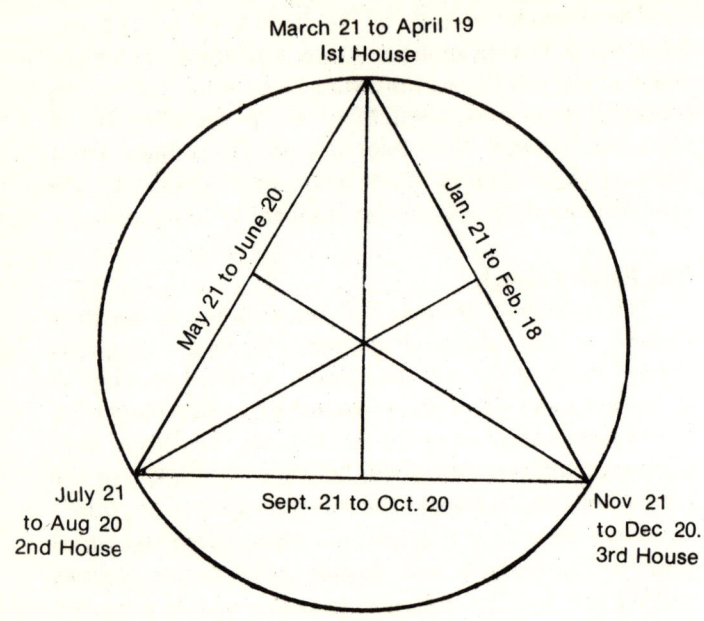

Fig. 6

THE FIRE TRIPLICITY
EXPLANATION
First House: March 21 to April 19 and "cusp" to April 26.
Second House: July 21 to August 20 and "cusp" to August 27.
Third House: November 21 to December 20 and "cusp" to December 27.
CENTRAL AFFINITIES
Of First House: September 21 to October 20 and "cusp" to October 27.
Of Second House: January 21 February 19 and "cusp" to February 26.
Of Third House: May 21 to June 20 and "cusp" to June 27.

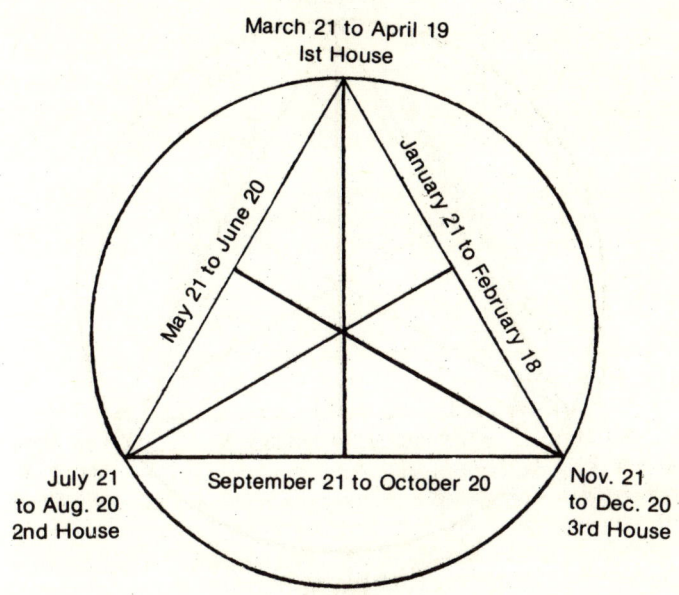

Fig. 7

THE WATER TRIPLICITY
EXPLANATION
First House: June 21 to July 20 and "cusp" to July 27.
Second House: October 21 to November 20 and "cusp" to November 27.
Third House: February 19 to March 20 and "cusp" to March 27.
CENTRAL AFFINITIES
Of First House: December 21 to January 20 and "cusp" to January 27.
Of Second House. April 20 to May 20 and "cusp" to May 27.
Of Third House: August 21 to September 20 and "cusp" to September 27.

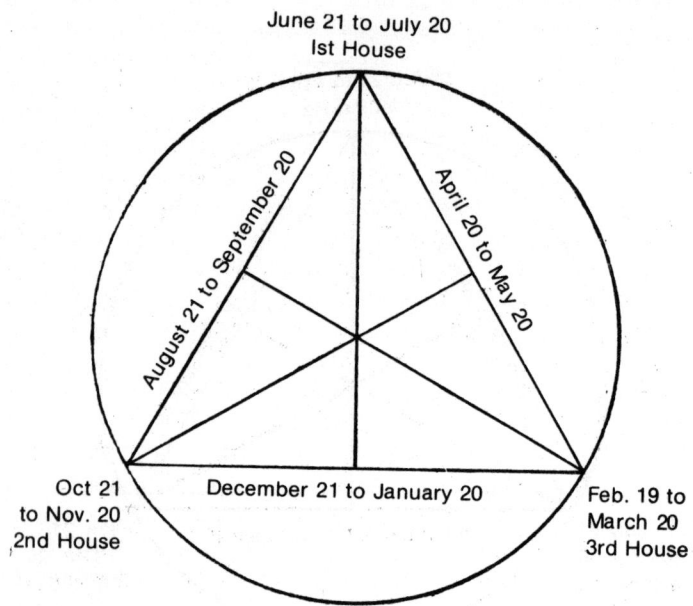

Fig. 8

THE AIR TRIPLICITY
EXPLANATION
First House: May 21 to June 20 and "cusp" to June 27.
Second House: September 21 to October 20 and "cusp" to October 27.
Third House: January 21 to February 19 and "cusp" to February 26.
CENTRAL AFFINITIES
Of First House: November 21 to December 20 and "cusp" to December 27.
Of Second House: March 21 to April 19 and "cusp" to April 26.
Of Third House: July 21 to August 20 and "cusp" to August 27.

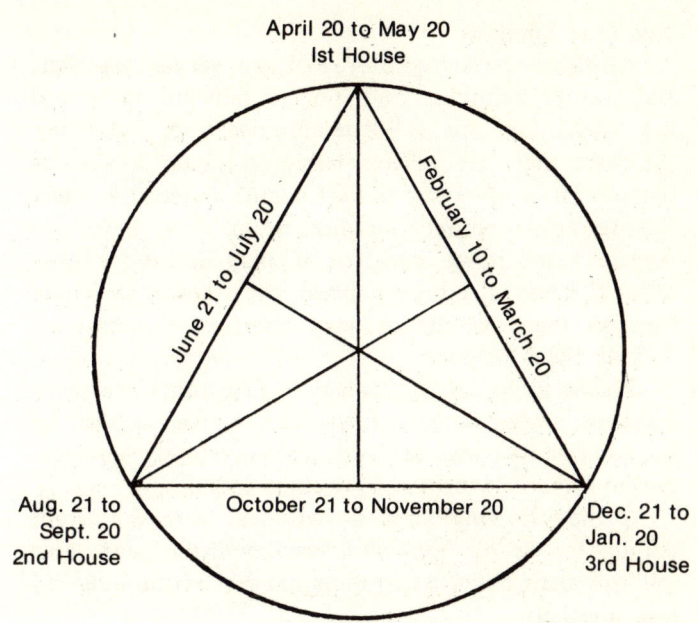

Fig. 9

THE EARTH TRIPLICITY
EXPLANATION
First House: April 20 to May 20 and "cusp" to May 27.
Second House: August 21 to September 20 and "cusp" to September 27.
Third House: December 21 to January 20 and "cusp" to January 27.

CENTRAL AFFINITIES
Of First House: October 21 to November 20 and "cusp" to November 27.

Of Second House: February 19 to March 20 and "cusp" to March 27.

Of Third House: June 21 to July 20 and "cusp" to July 27.

make it fruitful.

Not True Affinities

All these cases cited may, as I say, get on together, and even be helpful to one another; but still these are not what one can call true affinities, and, such being the case, they are always liable to separate, whereas those born on the same triangles, and especially when having the sympathetic numbers when once they come together can never part, or if they do (under some unusual stress of circumstances) they generally come together again in spite of every influence that may try to keep them asunder.

People under the symbolism of Fire and Water will, however, never blend, and if forced to live together by necessity or marriage they will just as certainly separate, and are likely in the end to become enemies.

In the following chapter I will deal with the exact colours for people born on every day of the year, and tell how their colours and numbers are harmonious to one another.

27

Lucky Colours
and How to Know Them

I WILL NOW PROCEED to explain how the vibrations of colours and numbers go together, an explanation which, I think my readers will find of the utmost use in many ways.

True Vibrations

No matter how beautiful a piano, harp, or other musical instrument may be to look at, if the vibration of its strings is not in accordance with its proper scale, the instrument will be considered out of tune *and useless for all practical purposes.*

It is the same with human beings; if their vibrations are not true in the harp of life, their thoughts and actions will cause discords and the unseen force of Nature prefers to leave them silent, or inactive, *rather than have inharmony in the great scheme of harmony,* which it has always been and ever will be Nature's purpose to attain.

As time is of so little importance to Nature, it follows that she does not worry about such infinitesimal things as human lives, with their odd threescore years and ten of sorrow or happiness. But to the human being his span of life is of the greatest importance; it is thus compulsory for us *to learn Nature's secrets as quickly and as early as possible, so that we may fit in with her plan* instead of demanding that Nature take that trouble for us, which I find so many people expect.

Without going further into his question, I will now proceed to show what are the principal colours associated with each birth number and month of birth.

How to Use Colours

Although the earth would look far brighter if we were to dress in our true colours in ordinary life, as do the flowers of the earth, yet, as I cannot expect to effect this drastic change all at once in our conventional appearance, I must content myself with hoping that my readers may commence to make the changes I suggest in some slight form, or at least in those working rooms or studios where they evolve their plans, write their letters or see their friends. If they do even this I honestly believe they will see quickly the advantage they will gain in their material success and also in their own personal happiness.

Colours of the Number 1

Persons born under the sign of the number 1, such as on the 1st, 10th, 19th, or 28th of any month, have for their main number, as I stated in previous chapters, the 1-4; and they can blend or use their colours with those given to the number 2-7, and vice versa. The 1-4 and 2-7 are the only double numbers that have to be considered in this way. The number 1-4 and its colours are more important to all those born in the "House of the 1-4," namely, from July 21-28 to August 20-28.

Their main colours are all shades from the palest yellow to deep orange or golden hues, and they can also use the colours of the 2-7, which are all shades from the palest green to the darkest, also creams and whites. All purples, blues, crimsons, and rose colours are favourable to them, *but they are not what are called the main colours*, and should only be used as accessories

The number 1 people should have as much as possible of the main colours around them, at least in their rooms or studios and in their dress, and they should also wear topaz or amber as much as possible in their jewellery.

Colours of the Number 2

The persons who have this number for their Birth Number are all those who are born on the 2nd, 11th, or 29th of any month, but this number and colour are of still more importance if they are born in what is called the "House of the 2-7." namely from June 21 to July 20-27.

Their main colours are all shades from the palest green to the darkest creams and whites, but they also can use the colours of the 1-4 sign as described above. Rose and pink tints and pale blues are also favourable to them, but only accessory colours, and the number 2 people should endeavour to wear and use all the lighter shades and *avoid deep tones of colour as much as possible*. The stones favourable for them to wear are pearls, cat's-eyes, and moonstones.

Colours of the Number 3

The persons who have this number for their Birth Number are all those born on the 3rd, 12th, 21st, or 30th of any month, but this number and colour are of still more significance if they are born in what is called the "House of the 3," namely from February 19 to March 20-27 or from November 21 to December 20-27.

Their main colours are all shades of mauve, violet, and purple, which they should have around them in their rooms or with them as much as possible, and they should also wear some jewel containing an amethyst. on account of its colour vibrations.

All shades of blue, crimson, or rose and yellow are

favourable for them, but only as accessories.

Colours of the Number 4

The persons who have this number for their Birth Number are all those who are born on the 4th, 13th, 22nd, or 31st of any month, but this number and colour are of still more significance if they are born either from July 21 to August 20-27, or from January 21 to February 19-26.

Their main colours are all shades of grey and fawn, and electric shades and the minor tints of yellow and green. They would also find the sapphire the most favourable stone to wear, on account of its colour vibrations.

Colours of the Number 5

The persons who have this number for their Birth Number are all those who are born on the 5th, 14th, or 23rd of any month, but this number and colour are of still greater significance if people are born in what is called the "House of the 5," namely, from May 21 to June 20-27, or from August 21 to September 20-27.

Their main or principal colours are all shades of silver grey, glistening white, or silvered, glittering materials, and as accessory colours *the pale or light shades of all colours.*

These people are far more magnetic if they do not wear or surround themselves with major colours or dark shades. They should also wear some jewel or ornament made of platinum or silver and diamonds, if possible.

Colours of the Number 6

The persons who have this number for their Birth Number are all those who are born on the 6th, 15th, or 24th of any month, but this number and its colours have greater significance for all those born in what is called the "House of the 6," namely from April 20 to May 20-27, or from September 21 to October 20-27.

Their main colours are all shades of blue, from the lightest to the darkest. *They have more accessory colours than any other class, and their range runs through all colours except black and dark purple.*

The turquoise and emeralds are the most favourable stones for these persons to wear, on account of their colour vibrations.

Colours of the Number 7

The persons who have this number for their Birth Number are all those who are born on the 7th, 16th or 25th of any month, but especially if they happen also to be born in what is called the "House of the 7-2"— namely, from June 21 to July 20-27. Their main colours are exactly similar to those given to people born under the number 2, which I described a little earlier, with this difference—that, as *they are more positive in character* than the number 2 people, so can they also wear stronger or more positive colours, but all shades of green and yellow remain their foundation or principal colours.

The jewels most personal and most favourable to them are moonstones, all white stones, and cat's-eyes, but these people should remember to avoid deep or dark colours, buth in stones and materials.

Colours of the Number 8

The persons who have this number for their Birth Number are all those who are born on the 8th, 17th, or 26th of any month, but especially if they happen also to be born in what is called the "House of the 8," namely, from December 21 to January 20-27, or from January 27 to February 19-26.

The first mentioned period is the Positive of their

number, while the second is the Negative.

These people, with their invariably strong personality, should be exceptionally careful of their surroundings and of their colours.

These seem "out of place" and irritable when surrounded by light, bright, or garish, tones, and they easily become silent, moody, and despondent under such circumstance.

As they are at heart grave, serious, and solid people, they should remember that all grave and serious colours *are theirs by right of birth*.

Even children born under the influence of this number (which has always been considered the number of mystery), especially if they are also born in the "House of the 8," seem strangely "out of the picture" if dressed in light, garish colours—and as they grow up this becomes more and more accentuated. On the contrary, all dark shades suit them and seem in harmoney with their personality and with their "atmosphere."

They would be especially fortunate in all tones of dark greys, blues, browns, runset shades, and so forth.

For example, take some man belonging to this number, dress him in light clothes and he will immediately look like a baker out on a holiday; whereas put the same man *in the colours that belong to him*, and every one will speak of his personality and his charm.

In their houses or business offices the same rule will again apply. Such people look "at ease" and "at home" when surrounded by oak panels and dark woodwork, and equally "out of place" when some unthinking architect gives them a Louis XV background.

For the same reason the jewels most fortunate and favourable and for such types are *all dark stone* h as dull rubies, carbuncles. and, best of all, the deep-toned sapphire, which is most markedly the jewel of the number 8.

Colours of the Number 9

The persons who have this number for their Birth Number are all those who are born on the 9th, 18th, or 27th of any month, but this number and its colour are of still more significance if people are born in what is called the "House of the 9" namely, from March 21 to April 19-26, or from October 21 to November 20-27. Their main colours are all shades of crimson or red, and their accessory colours are rose and pink, but they are more fortunate when they avoid the darker shades of these colours. All shades of blue are, however, very favourable for them.

They should wear red stones, such as rubies, garnets, and bloodstones.

If people will follow even in some degree the rules I have given about numbers and colours, and head the information in the previous chapters, they will very quickly be astonished by the good results they will notice in their daily lives.

There is no guesswork or mere theory about the rules I have laid down. They have been, in the first place, taken from ancient writings of the highest authority, all the dross or superfluities weeded out of them, and experimented on by myself in thousands upon thousands of cases before I have allowed them to pass.

The law of the "vibrations of things" *is as great as the law of gravitation*. It has, however, a wider and higher scope, for it concerns our thoughts as well as our actions. Professor Proctor, in his great work on astronomy, has laid down the rule that not the slightest vibration in the smallest atom in the farthest planet of our solar system but is intimately felt and associated with our human life on this planet, and, although many of these vibrations may be beyond our limited observation, as colours beyond the ultra-red and the ultra-violet are beyond our range of vision, yet that is no proof that they are not equally as powerful as those we can more readily examine.

It is well-known fact that there are tones and vibrations in music that are beyond our range of hearing yet there are other animals that as readily perceive these sounds as we do those that come within our scope.

We receive light and heat only by a certain tension of vibration, and scientists have declared that even life s only a qustion of vibration—that when it falls below a certain point it ceases.

By following out the simple rules set forth in this book one comes into harmony with Nature, there is less friction, as it were, in the vibrations of the human machine, and so one *will be able to accomplish more and so become more successful*.

Success and happiness are, after all, the principal pivots on which so much depends, both for ourselves and for those with whom we are brought into contact in our short journey from the cradle to the grave.